YouTube
MARKETING
POWER

YouTube MARKETING POWER

How to Use Video to Find More Prospects, Launch Your Products, and Reach a Massive Audience

JASON G. MILES

NEW YORK   CHICAGO   SAN FRANCISCO
ATHENS   LONDON   MADRID
MEXICO CITY   MILAN   NEW DELHI
SINGAPORE   SYDNEY   TORONTO

3 4 5 6 7 8 9 10   QVS/QVS   19 18 17 16 15

ISBN 978-0-07-183054-6
MHID   0-07-183054-5

e-ISBN 978-0-07-183055-3
e-MHID   0-07-183055-3

Design by Lee Fukui and Mauna Eichner

Library of Congress Cataloging-in-Publication Data

Miles, Jason, 1970-
  YouTube marketing power : how to use video to find more prospects, launch your products, and reach a massive audience / by Jason Miles.
    pages cm
  ISBN 978-0-07-183054-6 (pbk.) — ISBN 0-07-183054-5 (pbk.) 1. YouTube (Electronic resource) 2. Internet marketing. 3. Internet advertising. 4. Internet videos. 5. Video tape advertising. I. Title.
  HF5415.1265.M5384 2014
  658.8'72—dc23

2013030881

For my beautiful family:
Cinnamon, Jordan, Makena, and Liberty.
Thank you for your love, support, and encouragement
through the book-writing process.

Contents

Part 2
GETTING STARTED SUCCESSFULLY

Part 3
THE SUCCESSFUL SETUP

Part 4
SOCIAL STRATEGIES ON YOUTUBE

Part 5
GENERATING REVENUE ON YOUTUBE

Acknowledgments

owe a special debt of gratitude to my agent, Marilyn Allen, for making this book possible. Marilyn, thank you for all you've done to help my writing career become a reality and for your help in making this book happen. Thank you, Janie Kliever, for all your help getting the manuscript ready. I could not do this without you. Finally, I want to thank my talented and beautiful cofounder at Liberty Jane Clothing, Cinnamon Miles. You put up with me through the worst of this project, and I'm truly grateful. I couldn't ask for a better partner in life.

Introduction

A New Version of American Life

My daughter walks into the kitchen before school and says, "Dad, let's watch *Good Mythical Morning* together. It's my new favorite show." I'm a little startled since, her being 14 and all, I'm not exactly cool to her anymore—if I ever was. So I jump at the chance to bond a bit and head toward the family room.

She turns on the TV, navigates to the show, and we start watching. I've got to admit; it's really funny. Two guys (as I discovered, they were the comedy duo Rhett & Link) comedians like the old-school duos of Andy Griffith and Don Knotts or Bill Murray and Dan Aykroyd. The show ended after just 12 minutes, which was a little odd, so we watch another one. I'm hooked.

The show we watched wasn't on ABC or NBC or even on a cable channel like Oxygen. She didn't navigate through our DVR-recorded shows to find it. It was on YouTube—she navigated to YouTube and effortlessly started the show. We watched it on our TV, full screen, in HD, just like we'd watch any other show. Times have changed.

It's said that YouTube killed TV, but the truth is, YouTube killed TV's monopoly on video distribution. Rhett McLaughlin and Link Neal have an amazing show, and they have 1.2 million subscribers on their primary YouTube Channel and another 500,000 on their secondary channel. They produced *Good Mythical Morning* for several seasons, every morning, just like *The View* or *Live with Kelly & Michael*. They have an audience that puts them in the same league as prime-time TV shows. We'll learn more about Rhett & Link in Chapter 5 when we interview them to learn how they started on YouTube and how they approach their work.

In many ways, just as Amazon has reinvented the book publishing space, YouTube has reinvented the video production and distribution space. The ability to start a video production company in your garage (or more likely bedroom) is real. And marketers are leveraging YouTube in powerful new ways to expand their reach and strengthen their brands.

Imagine we're another three or four years down the road for a moment. What do you see YouTube's viewership being?

1. Greater than today?

2. Equal to today?

3. Less than today?

I'd guess we have the same opinion, that YouTube will have a much greater viewership in the future as the entire planet gets broadband Internet access.

What's your experience? I'm guessing:

- You're responsible for marketing your business.

- You're trying to understand how to identify and then pay for a steady stream of new prospects.

- You're a frequent user of YouTube, and you've seen YouTube be successful for other businesses. (Well, at least for that blender guy with his *Will It Blend?* videos.) But you wonder if it would work for your niche or industry.

In this book, we'll explore:

- Why YouTube is a huge opportunity for businesses

- Why companies frequently fail at YouTube marketing and how to fix faltering performances

- What are some effective styles of video making

- How to get your videos done quickly and easily

- How some of the best marketers on YouTube are creating massive followings

- How you can advertise on YouTube to drive traffic and revenue to your existing business

- How you can monetize your YouTube work and make real money by creating simple videos

This book will help you get past the roadblocks and barriers to effective YouTube marketing. So jump in and start creating your YouTube marketing plan today.

You Tube
MARKETING
POWER

THE POWER OF YOUTUBE

Chapter 1

YouTube Marketing Power

On April 23, 2005, Chad Hurley, Steve Chen, and Jawed Karim uploaded the first video onto their new video-sharing website—YouTube.com. The video was a brief clip titled *Me at the Zoo*. The goal of the new site was to make video sharing easy and to allow anyone to upload a video and share it with the world. To say they succeeded is an understatement.

The three former PayPal employees had been laboring away for months at their small office above Amici's Pizzeria on East Third Avenue in San Mateo, California. San Mateo is just south of San Francisco in the famed Silicon Valley. By May 2005, they were ready to offer the public a beta test of their new site. Then they officially opened the doors to all visitors in November of that year.

The site took off very quickly. It took the YouTube team just 12 months to scale from 50,000 monthly users to 17 million. That was the fastest growth rate of any website in the history of the Internet, and it has been eclipsed only by Pinterest, which did it in 9 months.

By 2006, more than 65,000 videos were being added daily to the site, and in October of that year, Google announced that it had purchased YouTube for $1.65 billion in Google stock. Just 19 months after uploading *Me at the Zoo*, the three founding partners joined Silicon Valley royalty as newly minted megamillionaires.

In November 2006, Salman Khan, a hedge fund analyst, set up a YouTube account to begin helping his cousins with their homework. He thought if he uploaded videos that they could use as a supplement to their homework, it might help them. Today the Khan Academy channel has over a million subscribers and has had over 270 million video views. The more than 2,200 videos on Salman's list teach everything from basic arithmetic to science. Bill Gates has said about the Khan Academy, "You've just got a glimpse of the future of education."

In January 2007, a young Canadian mom uploaded a video of her son singing in a local talent competition. Her 12-year-old son sang Ne-Yo's "So Sick." His name was Justin Bieber. YouTube allowed him to be discovered and helped launch his career. Two years later, his first album went platinum. Today, the official Justin Bieber YouTube channel has over 4.7 million subscribers and has had over 3.7 billion video views.

In 2010, YouTube gained additional recognition after it was reported that the site was receiving more than 2 billion video views a day. That number was estimated to be roughly twice the number achieved by all three major U.S. television networks combined. YouTube was bigger than television.

In 2011, YouTube reported that it had more than 1 trillion total video views. That is approximately 140 video views for every person on earth. The platform has become the number one video-hosting site online, the number two search engine behind Google, and one of the top social networking sites.

The popularity of the site has never declined. Eight years after launching, the company reached an incredible milestone—1 billion visitors a month come to the site and enjoy a staggering 4 billion hours of video.

Visitors watch YouTube videos locally in 1 of 53 countries and in 61 languages. As much as 70 percent of YouTube's traffic comes from outside the United States. The *Wall Street Journal* has reported that in 2012 the website generated an estimated $4 billion in revenue.

A New Marketing Option

From the beginning, entrepreneurial types saw the potential of YouTube for business. Some of those early adopters were large corporations, some were small businesses and entrepreneurs, and some were just creative video makers who saw an opportunity. This latter group realized they could monetize the traffic their videos would generate and created small video publishing businesses around different niche topics.

The early benefits of YouTube for business were obvious: the site offered a video-hosting service, a social network, and a search engine function, all in one. This level of utility, offered for free, caused a lot of speculation about whether the YouTube business model was sustainable. But YouTube's founders had learned the lessons first pioneered by Google—to give away real value in exchange for massive levels of user adoption that they would later monetize through advertising. However, once Google bought YouTube in 2006, fears about the company's sustainability faded.

In May 2007, YouTube debuted its Partner Program, which allowed users to generate revenue based on the AdSense advertising model. The concept was simple: upload a video, get lots of views, and earn some respectable money.

A Challenge for Businesses

Because YouTube has been incredibly well embraced by consumers, you would think that businesses large and small would have joined the party and figured out how to position themselves well on YouTube to grow their businesses. Oddly enough, by 2010, only 50 percent of the Fortune Global 100 brands had created a YouTube channel. By 2012 that number had jumped to 79 percent, according to research firm Burson-Marsteller. But many businesses still struggle to overcome the basic challenges of successful YouTube marketing. Although it's difficult to determine exactly what is holding so many businesses back, there are seven common reasons I believe are contributing to the failure to launch:

1. A lack of creative talent to produce engaging videos

2. A lack of enthusiasm for the format and a fear of being on camera

3. Internal bureaucracy and corporate friction that make it impossible to get interesting video content published

4. A fear of taking risks, which produces a bland, uninspired style of video and fails to attract any attention, serving as a self-fulfilling negative feedback loop

5. A fundamental misunderstanding of the site's purpose (many business owners believe it's either simply a video-hosting site or not a good match for their marketing efforts)

6. Failure to clarify a marketing strategy that will work on the YouTube platform

7. An inability to embrace new online video standards and allow videos to be made with lower production values but higher engagement values

POWER TIP

Identify and overcome the roadblocks within your company that are holding you back from developing an exciting YouTube marketing strategy.

Our Journey on YouTube

We started our small business in February 2008 on our kitchen table. We began as an eBay store, selling custom doll clothes at auction. It was a humble beginning. My wife's first custom outfit sold for $39, and we were hooked. Our goal was to do everything we could to improve our auction results.

When we were just starting out, we didn't understand all the potential that YouTube held for our business, but we did want a video-hosting tool so we could make simple videos to promote our new products. Our small business was fairly simple, and we knew videos could help us get it off the ground. My wife would make new designs, and we'd auction them on eBay. As part of the auction listing format, if you know a little HTML, you can embed a video from YouTube that people can play right in the eBay listing. That seemed like a fairly good way to create a competitive advantage and get people to engage with our products. So we made our first video in August 2008, just in time for the launch of our fall line.

We soon realized that YouTube was more than a video-hosting site. People started to comment on and like our videos on YouTube. We had assumed people would just watch them on eBay in the product listing— that YouTube was far too vast for anyone to notice our odd little doll-related videos. But we were wrong. We began to discover that there was a large community of 13-year-old girls on YouTube who still loved American Girl dolls—the type of customer my wife designed her clothes for. They would comment on, like, and share our videos.

We had discovered the social side of YouTube. It offered a social networking element that allowed us to engage with prospects in an exciting way. This level of engagement beyond eBay was incredibly energizing for us. It made us realize that we could cultivate a social following online that would support our eBay sales.

We started to brainstorm ways we could engage with our newfound friends on YouTube. We discovered that contests worked incredibly well for our audience (we'll cover how to run contests later). Our contests are very simple. We ask people to design a doll outfit and make a video about it, and we pick a winner based on her design skills. For the prize, we make the outfit and send it to the winner for free. We've run this type of contest every year for five years. In our most successful contest, we received over 2,400 video entries and over 19,000 video views.

Today, we have more than 10,000 subscribers on our YouTube channel and more than 1.8 million video views. YouTube is consistently one of the top sources of traffic to our e-commerce site, http://www.liberty janepatterns.com.

Our most successful video to date, a simple how-to tutorial, has over 50,000 video views. We've published over 250 videos in the last five years. Most have just a few thousand views. A few have over 50,000 views. One has over 100,000 views. But all of them are working hard for us by positioning us with our ideal prospects.

But our videos aren't just watched frequently; they also accumulate responses from viewers. In our video category, "Howto & Style," we created 6 of the top 50 most-responded-to videos of all time, which is an incredible result. You can see those stats on the third-party analysis site VidStatsX at http://vidstatsx.com/most-responded-how-to-style -videos-all-time. Just look for our "spokesgirl" Liberty. You'll see that there isn't anyone else in our category who has this type of success.

We've taken the lessons learned on YouTube and leveraged them on other social platforms, including Facebook, Pinterest, and Instagram. We're proud of what we've accomplished over the last five years with our YouTube channel. But our efforts are a tiny success story compared with the stories of many others who have achieved astounding success on the platform. We'll share their stories throughout this book.

Our Goals on YouTube

You might be wondering what our marketing plan for YouTube looks like. Let me outline the basic elements right up front and then unpack these concepts over the course of this book. Our original marketing strategy included six steps and expanded to these eight:

1. We began our work by simply creating videos that we could use in our eBay listings. This strategy was aimed at giving us a competitive edge on eBay. People would see one of our listings, skim it briefly, and then notice a video embedded. The video was simply more product photography set to music. It also allowed the eBay shoppers to see our YouTube channel name and connect with us outside eBay.

2. When we realized there was an eager audience on YouTube ready to watch our videos, we began making videos for them, asking them to comment on and like our videos as well as subscribe to our channel.

3. We created design contests that engaged our community. We asked viewers to create a video as their method of responding to the contest, and we promised to give them a terrific prize.

4. We began leveraging YouTube's "Call-to-Action overlay" feature on our videos to help drive traffic to our e-commerce site and brand ourselves more strongly on YouTube.

5. We learned to use YouTube's "Promoted Videos" feature to gain viewers and subscribers. We run these specifically when we have a big contest under way.

6. We began strategically embedding videos in our sales pages on our website, http://www.libertyjaneclothing.

7. We discovered that people love how-to and tutorial videos and began making them for our audience.

8. We learned to use the YouTube Partner Program to earn additional income from the advertising that runs on our videos. Although this isn't our primary objective, it does provide a small ongoing stream of income that helps grow our business.

You might be thinking that none of these steps sound very difficult or overly clever, and you're right. They are not rocket science. The marketing tactics we use on YouTube are designed to give our customers a good video-watching experience, bond them to our brand, and set ourselves apart from the competition. None of that takes tricks or gimmicks or secret tactics. It simply takes a consistent and determined approach.

Finding Your Way to Business Benefits

There are countless YouTube success stories in every possible industry. The real question is: Are you going to be one of them? You probably fall into one of these three categories:

1. You've never tried YouTube, and you're skeptical, but you're looking for another marketing channel and are willing to give it a try.

2. You tried YouTube and didn't seem to find any success. Maybe you have a channel that is languishing with a handful of subscribers and no social engagement, and you suffer from a lack of dedication to creating new videos. There are literally millions of small businesses in this category.

3. You're on YouTube and consider it a successful marketing channel, but you want to find more success and discover new marketing techniques.

Finding your way toward a successful YouTube marketing strategy starts with the realization that there are barriers and obstacles that you need to overcome. When you do, you'll realize a set of business benefits that are incredibly potent. In the next chapter, we'll dive deeply into the business benefits of YouTube, but let me briefly mention them now.

A successful YouTube marketing strategy will result in the following business benefits:

1. **Traffic to your website.** Effective video marketing allows you to drive traffic to your primary e-commerce site. This happens through the links placed in your video descriptions and on your channel page. Once viewers are on your website, you can sell your products, sign people up for your newsletter, or get them to jump into your other social media platforms to discover more about your brand.

2. **Bonding opportunities with prospects.** When you create effective videos that meet your target market's needs, you position yourself to truly bond with new prospects. Your brand becomes memorable in a way much more powerfully than via print. People will bond with your brand and appreciate that you've made a video that will help them, make them laugh, or educate them about a topic.

3. **A product launch resource.** When you create videos in conjunction with a new product, you give your prospects and customers another way to experience your new product or service. The video might explain the product in a way that a print piece or simple product description never could.

4. **Search engine assets.** When you make a video, you benefit from exposure on the top two search engines online. First, Google indexes YouTube videos and displays them prominently when people search for your topic or keyword. YouTube itself is the second leading search engine behind Google. People go to YouTube and search for a topic. Your video could be just the thing they are looking for, and they'll become exposed to you and your brand.

5. **A social media platform.** YouTube is a social media platform. It is commonly left off the lists of top social media sites, but it is a powerful platform. There is no doubt that on YouTube, people subscribe, like, and comment. You can engage with these people and build real rapport and friendship.

6. **A video-hosting service.** Before YouTube, if you wanted to have videos hosted online, you'd have to pay for that privilege. YouTube

offers it for free. You can host videos on YouTube, then embed them on your website and many other sites, such as eBay.

7. **An advertising channel.** YouTube offers several ways to advertise to find new customers. And the beautiful part is that it is incredibly cost-effective. It's a little-known secret that advertising on YouTube is incredibly inexpensive, because the site's advertising platform is not as popular as Facebook or Google AdWords. In fact, in Part 5 of the book, I'll show you how to get ad traffic from YouTube for free.

And Action!

(1) Identify the underlying reasons why your business might not be on YouTube and start discussing them with key stakeholders. (2) Audit the state of your current YouTube work and find out if you have a channel. Maybe your company has a channel that you don't even know about. (3) Resolve to address the issues and overcome the obstacles holding you back. (4) Think about how your business can benefit from a successful YouTube marketing plan and begin to create goals and objectives to achieve that success.

24 Business Benefits of YouTube Marketing

The business benefits of a well-coordinated YouTube marketing plan shouldn't be overlooked or glossed over. Maybe you're an entrepreneur and you're trying to decide if YouTube is worth your time and energy. Maybe you're on a marketing team at your company and you need to convince your bosses that a YouTube strategy will work for your business. Whatever your reason for picking up this book, let's look at the business reasons why you need a YouTube marketing plan.

But before we start, let me just mention what should be obvious: there is no bigger waste of time for busy executives than toiling toward vague social media goals with no clear link to business outcomes. For me and our business, if the social media platform doesn't directly relate to a business objective, then I don't want to spend the time or energy on it. So let's look at business outcomes and the specific benefits that can be easily derived from thoughtful YouTube marketing.

Traffic to Your Website from YouTube

I have to assume that your website is an e-commerce site where people can buy your product or (at a minimum) learn more about product or service offerings. The math is simple. The more qualified traffic you get, the greater your volume of prospects who will agree to purchase. Let's look at a few ways YouTube helps send traffic to your website.

Search Engine Optimization

Google, Bing, and Yahoo serve up content each time someone searches for a specific keyword. Frequently, one of the top results they serve is a video. When you create YouTube videos, you're automatically creating content that is highly useful for the search engines. They will find you. Do this well enough for your niche or industry, and you can start to divert a healthy stream of search traffic from the search engines to your YouTube page and ultimately to your products or services. Another way consumers search these days is by searching for a keyword in Google, then clicking on the Video tab to see what video responses pop up.

Video Search Optimization

Internet searchers aren't as unsophisticated as they used to be. YouTube became the second most popular search engine for one simple reason. People ask themselves a question before initiating a search: Am I looking for a video or text result? Frequently, they know they are looking for a video result. Maybe it's the new Justin Bieber video. Maybe it's a Photoshop tutorial. Maybe it's a guide to learning "God Bless America" on the bass guitar. People are sophisticated about searching, and when they search on YouTube for a video about your product, niche, or industry, are they going to find you? If they do, then the traffic landing on your YouTube channel will educate them about your brand and product options.

Referral Traffic from Videos

Each video you make has a description field that allows a clickable link that can take people to your website or product page. While you can't place a clickable link to an external website directly on your video, you can make a clickable link to another YouTube video. Make it your goal to ensure that each video you produce has a description and a link back to your website or a relevant product. Make the link the first item in the description so that it is prominently displayed.

Referral Traffic from Your YouTube Channel

Most visitors to your videos will click over to your channel and check out your overall presentation. This is when your channel strategy needs to engage them. This is the moment of truth. They'll look to see how many subscribers and videos you have and whether you have links to your website or other social media sites. Your YouTube channel is like a portal that offers options to take people to these various locations.

Referral Traffic from Call-to-Action Overlays

One of the simplest methods for generating solid traffic to your website is the use of a Call-to-Action overlay (see Figure 2.1). Not only is this method of advertising easy to set up, but it's also cheap. In fact, in Chapter 16, we'll show you how to make it virtually free. The possibilities are endless, and the opportunities to drive traffic from your video to your website are simple and easy.

Figure 2.1 The Call-to-Action overlay allows you to advertise on your videos.

Social Discovery on YouTube

I use the term *social discovery* to refer to the process of being found on social networks and also of finding new prospects on social networks. This should be a key part of your marketing efforts. You want your best customers to engage with you so that their friends and like-minded contacts see them interact with your brand. You want them to discover you through their friends. How many times have you heard a new customer say, "I am so glad I found you"? *Answer:* Not often enough! But your chances of being found by your ideal customers go way up when you're effectively using YouTube. Here is how.

Comments and Conversations

When you speak with prospective customers through comments, you have an opportunity to influence them toward your products and services. But it's even better when prospective customers comment on your videos and your loyal customers respond for you. Their energy and support are incredibly compelling. Third-party endorsements are much stronger than you directly representing claims about your products or services. But don't worry; YouTube is not as conversation intensive as Facebook. You can post a video and check it regularly for comments, but generally speaking, they are not too overwhelming.

Social Sharing

When loyal fans share your videos either within YouTube on their playlists or on other social networks like Facebook, LinkedIn, or Twitter, they help spread the news about you and your brand. Likewise, when bloggers take your videos and embed them into their blog posts, your reach is broadened. This type of social sharing extends your reach throughout your niche or industry and helps to build your name awareness.

Subscribing to Your Channel

When people subscribe to your channel, they see your videos in their home feeds. That means that the more subscribers you have, the more people are going to easily find your next video. But subscribers to your channel play another key role—social proof. Are you a big deal? Well, 10,000 subscribers on YouTube is pretty good proof. So the more people you have subscribing to your YouTube channel, the more your videos will be viewed, and the more social proof you'll have when prospects visit your channel for the first time.

Contest Participation

The biggest benefit of running a contest on YouTube is that your fans and followers get to engage deeply with your brand by making a video entry. They spend hours making a video to enter your contest. Then they upload it to YouTube, and it is shared with all their friends. Regardless of whether they win or not, they have shared your brand with all their contacts. Imagine if 1,000 people enter your contest and each of them has 100 subscribers on their YouTube channel. Your brand will have been placed in front of 100,000 high-quality prospects.

Fan Videos

If you can cultivate your brand to the point where customers make fan videos, then you've done a powerful thing. We are fortunate enough to have fan videos frequently made and shared on YouTube. The most common type of fan video is of customers excitedly opening their Liberty Jane Clothing packages. They share that moment with their friends via video. Yes, this really happens regularly. You can see our collection of fan videos at http://pinterest.com/cinnamonmiles/seen-wearing -liberty-jane/. Of course, all it takes is getting one of these, which you promote heavily, for others to begin pouring in.

Referral Traffic to Other Social Channels

Your YouTube channel is a great place to add links to your other social networks. When people click onto your channel page, they'll look to see if you have links to your website or other social channels. On occasion, it's wise to also mention your other social networks in your videos, too. You want to cross-pollinate as much as possible so that people follow you on various social networks. That way, if they abandon YouTube, they still have a connection to you via other social networks.

Selling Goods and Services

There is no better reason to be on social media than to make direct sales. People will tell you that selling via social networks will not work—those people are wrong. You can sell your products effectively using YouTube. You can use the platform throughout the sales cycle, from discovery all the way through to product guarantee and new-buyer support. Consider the following selling methods.

Video as a General Sales Tool

You have a very simple way to improve your product pages. Make a sales-related video and embed it in your sales page. This "rich media" has been clearly shown to improve your sales rates. For one thing, it keeps people on your product page longer. It also allows you to explain the benefits of your product in a conversational tone. Finally, it gives people an opportunity to evaluate your sincerity and the level of professionalism of your company.

> **POWER TIP**
>
> Maximize your use of video by hosting it on YouTube, embedding it on your website, and sharing it on social media sites such as Facebook and Pinterest.

How-to Videos

Does your product support a complex activity? Maybe you make sewing machine oil or cooking utensils. If you make a product that is part of a larger activity, then demonstrate that activity and show how your product helps make it easy. Maybe your product is complicated to install, unpack, put together, or begin using. A simple how-to video on YouTube can be a fantastic tool to help supplement your other sales materials. These videos can be placed on YouTube and then shared on your other social channels, like Facebook and Pinterest. You can also embed them on your website to support the sales cycle.

Customer Support Tool

Do you frequently get customer service inquiries that can best be explained with a video? Are there commonly misunderstood aspects of your product or service? You can make a collection of customer support videos and host them on YouTube, then also embed them in your website's FAQ section. Customers will appreciate the rich-media content. It will also allow you to bond with your customers as they work through their challenges. The greatest possible use of these videos is to establish the rapport and respect necessary for them to say, "I want to buy from these guys again."

Tutorials for Your Customers

Do you have a product that is challenging to learn how to use? Maybe it's software, or perhaps it's a tool or solution that has multiple steps. Creating tutorials to train your customers on how best to use your product is a natural way to use YouTube. This option is particularly useful for business-to-business sellers looking to support other businesses as they work with clients. The more you bond with them and support them in the sales process with their customers, the more they'll look to you as a trusted partner.

Product Demonstrations

Do you have a product that must be seen to be believed? Maybe simply showing your product in action is enough to win new customers. Consider your product's greatest strength or benefit and determine how to show it off in a well-created video. One of the most famous product demonstrations on YouTube is from the folks at Blendtec with their famous slogan, "Will it blend? That is the question." Then they proceed to show their blender blending everything you can possibly imagine, from iPhones to baseballs. Their creative product demonstrations turned their tiny company into a global brand.

Formal Testimonials

Do you have a celebrity or well-known industry veteran who will speak about your product, service, or company? Having the testimonial recorded on video gives you multiple media options in one. You can play it as a video on YouTube and other online platforms. You can strip the audio out and use it in formats such as radio spots. Or you can simply take the testimonial and transcribe it for use in print pieces.

Coupons or Discount Offers

One way to boost your number of YouTube subscribers is to occasionally offer a special coupon or discount exclusively through YouTube. Make sure it is a limited-time offer, and leave it posted. Even though people have missed the opportunity to use the coupon, they'll learn that subscribing to your channel is a wise move.

Money-Back Guarantee Method

Do you want a way to boost the strength and selling power of your return policy or money-back guarantee? Shoot a video explaining it that starts with something like, "Hi, I'm [insert your name], the president of [insert company name], and I'd like to personally explain our money-back guarantee." That will put life back into this tired sales tool.

Buyer Bonus—Free Videos

Do you have a product that can be enhanced by a buyer bonus of free training videos? Do you need a way to enhance your offer? Making a collection of buyer bonus videos is easy. You can simply host them on YouTube and then e-mail a link as part of your receipting or thank you process.

Brand Building

Ultimately, your brand is the most important business asset you can have, and if developed well, it can add massive value. YouTube allows you to position yourself, compare yourself with your competitors, and strengthen the name awareness of your brand and products in the marketplace. Here are a few of the opportunities available.

Product Placement

On YouTube, you have an opportunity to have your products placed in other people's videos, not just your own. Are there industry veterans or celebrities who make videos? You can simply approach them about including your product in their videos. We do this at Liberty Jane Clothing by giving popular video makers free clothing items that they use in their stop-motion videos. Simply give them a product sample and ask them to include your brand name in the video description (see Figure 2.2).

Figure 2.2 Including your products in other people's popular videos is a natural way to get greater brand exposure.

Greater Name Awareness

Are you an unknown competitor in your industry? Looking to break into the minds of prospective consumers? A general positioning video on YouTube can help. You can place it on your channel and then advertise it on YouTube to further its reach toward your target customers.

Positioning Tool

Do you need to position yourself in a unique way vis-à-vis your competition? A well-made YouTube video can be an effective tool in highlighting your unique selling proposition and setting yourself apart from the competition.

Conclusions

There is no shortage of business uses for YouTube. The only question is, will you take the time to creatively brainstorm the ways in which YouTube can be adapted to your business needs? From advertising to customer service, YouTube can be a powerful part of your business toolkit.

One of the most important things you can do is document your lessons learned and share your insights with your coworkers. If you try to use YouTube for one business purpose and it fails, document the reason why and try something else. Ultimately, your successes will be the result of experimentation and discovery.

And Action!

(1) Identify the top five benefits of using YouTube for your business. (2) Work to implement them in an organized way. (3) Monitor the real business results and document your lessons learned. (4) Take the time and energy to ensure your brainstorming includes areas involving traffic, social discovery, selling goods and services, and brand building.

Why Companies Fail at YouTube Marketing

I t doesn't take long to look for examples of very well-known companies that totally fail at YouTube marketing. Do a little digging into the elite companies in your niche or industry and ask yourself the following question: Do they do a terrible job at YouTube marketing? And the most important question to ask yourself is this: Is my company really awful at YouTube marketing? The answer is frequently yes.

The Corporate Challenges

Unlike Facebook, which most companies seem to be able to figure out easily enough, YouTube marketing has some land mines that can maim even the best guerrilla marketers. So you'll see shocking examples of both success and failure everywhere on the site. You'll see some companies that have marched forward to victory and others that are casualties of war. This latter group won't even acknowledge YouTube as a social network. I refer to this phenomenon as "YouTube blindness." Sadly, many marketers have it.

You can take this investigation further by looking at media personalities, top-ranked authors, and Fortune 500 companies. Many times, they will not have a YouTube channel at all. When they do, you will frequently find that their YouTube channels have the following disastrous characteristics:

- **A handful of random videos that don't have a clear mission or purpose.** You're left with the feeling that either this is just a place they host videos that they use somewhere else, or they don't have a real reason they are using YouTube.

- **Featured videos on their channels that are poor quality and not engaging.** Many times, the piece is a promotional product video or a company overview that doesn't grab your attention.

- **Videos with very low view counts.** This leaves you with the impression that the video isn't worth watching. Oddly enough, people watch what other people watch. So a low view count is negative social proof and will repel potential viewers.

- **A very low subscribership.** When you see a massive A-list brand with very low subscriber numbers on YouTube, you know the brand doesn't have an effective marketing plan. It's more negative social proof and creates a negative feedback loop where prospects come and visit but don't subscribe.

- **Just a few video or channel comments.** This leaves you with the impression that no one is watching, no one is showing up, no one is talking, and no one cares.

But it doesn't have to be that way. All of us have seen examples of 10-year-old kids putting videos on YouTube and getting millions of video views and tens of thousands of subscribers. How can youngsters so easily outgun Fortune 500 marketers? How can these amateur YouTube users effortlessly attract millions of watchers, while the marketing professionals with MBAs struggle to take advantage of the site?

I'm That Guy

You've heard my story about Liberty Jane Clothing and our YouTube channel (http://www.youtube.com/libertyjaneclothing), but I also serve as Vice President of Advancement at Northwest University, a terrific Christian university in the Seattle area. When I took over responsibility for the university's marketing functions, I inherited a YouTube channel strategy that hadn't been used well. The channel (http://www.youtube.com/northwestuniversity) had:

- A handful of subscribers

- A handful of video views

- Very few video or channel comments

- A featured video that hadn't been changed in years—and that had very few views

- No system or pipeline of video production

- No vision or plan for how to use the YouTube channel to engage with people

I'd love to tell you that I flipped a few switches and made a few minor requests of the marketing team, and we instantly got our YouTube work rolling. But the truth is, it's been a painfully slow journey toward creating something that we can all be proud of and that engages people in a creative way. It was reality check time. I learned that it is one thing to find YouTube success as a small business owner or entrepreneur and another thing entirely to find success inside a large corporation or entity.

The problem I encountered at Northwest wasn't that we had a bad marketing team. We had truly brilliant, creative talent and gifted marketers. I'm proud to work with a team that has incredible trade skill in all the creative areas. The problem wasn't that we didn't have money; we had the funds to do the work. Nor was the problem that we didn't know what to do; I clearly knew what would and wouldn't work on YouTube. The truth is that institutional- or corporate-level YouTube work is just more complicated.

Why Entrepreneurs Have It Easier

Why is it harder to implement a YouTube marketing strategy in a larger corporate context and easier to implement in a smaller context? Here are a few reasons.

Faster Speed of Learning

In the smaller business context, you can make creative decisions, implement them immediately, test your results, and learn how to improve very quickly. In larger corporate settings, you usually cannot execute quickly, and the cycle of improvement slows to a painful crawl.

Tighter Focus on Your Audience

In a smaller company, you generally have one focus—serving your customers. In a larger company, suddenly more random people begin to matter. In a university, for example, you have prospective students who are your core prospects, but alumni and donors are also an important audience. This diffused focus makes implementation more challenging.

Less Bureaucratic Approval

In a smaller company, you can get approval, explain the goal, and rally support for the plan in 20 or 30 minutes. In a larger corporate context, this can take months as you work to gain both staff-level buy-in and senior management buy-in. You can run your ship aground on either side of that equation. And if you hit resistance or political infighting from key internal stakeholders, you can be in decision purgatory for a very long time.

Rewards for Risk Taking

At Liberty Jane Clothing, when we want to try a new video approach or style, we say, "What the heck—our [viewers] might really like it." And bam, we do it. If our peeps do indeed like it, we've found a new way to engage with them and grow our influence and reach. Sales increase, and our small business grows that much closer to our goals. If the people in our audience don't like the new video format, then we don't really worry about it. All we've wasted was the time and energy it took to make the video and place it on YouTube. We've lost nothing. But in a corporate context, when a person has to be assigned to make a video, the stakes are higher. At a minimum, if the video fails on any level, people will feel like their time and talent were wasted or like they are being judged neg-atively for their creative execution. They'll resent the assignment. Man-agers will feel like money was wasted, and senior leaders will worry that the marketing team doesn't know what it's doing. All this happens even if you tell people you want them to experiment and try new things, even if you give them permission to fail.

Effective Creative Execution

When radio came out a hundred years ago, marketers found a creative approach that worked well by trial and error. When television came out, the same thing happened. Practitioners learn what works and refine it over time. The same is true for YouTube. The style of video that is ef-fective on YouTube is not complex, nor is it in need of expensive (high-end) production values. It is simple, engaging, personable, and—most importantly—fun or interesting or both. But many "old-school" mar-keters haven't spent enough time on YouTube as watchers to get their bearings straight and pick up on this nuance. Small business marketers don't have the money for high production values and expensive video shoots, so they don't do them. And fortunately for them, that fits with the effective creative execution that works well on YouTube. As an en-trepreneur, you pick up your camera, point it at your smiling face, make your video, and publish it. Your tribe is happy. It's a simple affair. In a corporate context, when you pay someone to make a video, you fre-quently end up with overscripted, overedited, overpriced videos that fail to engage in an authentic, friendly, and simple way.

Clearly, you can have the dream team of marketers but still fail to launch an effective YouTube marketing strategy. Obviously, that is what is hap-pening at the Fortune 500 companies we identified earlier. These com-panies have great marketers, probably whole office towers full of them, but the barriers of corporate culture prevent YouTube success.

Some of the barriers I've personally encountered on my journey as a vice president in charge of marketing include:

- No one on the marketing team with a background in or knowledge of how to do YouTube marketing or with the assigned responsibil-ity to make it happen.

- Video people who wanted overscripted, overedited, and over-thought videos without a vision or plan for the overall YouTube strategy.

- A long list of priorities that were honestly more urgent or pressing than getting the YouTube marketing plan set up.

- A difficult time coming up with a creative video approach that everyone could rally around.

- Confusion over who should be responsible for the YouTube channel. The social media team? The webmaster? The IS department?

- Videographers who didn't want to consider the social media- or advertising-related aspects of YouTube.

- Trouble finding a videographer whom we could work with effectively and afford.

- Videographers who didn't listen to instructions and created videos that were unusable.

- Weakness in other social media areas that made it difficult to jump-start our YouTube work. In essence, if e-mail marketing and Facebook marketing are both areas of weakness, then launching a YouTube strategy is going to be more challenging.

- Staffers who were afraid to take risks or be creative for fear that I'd be unhappy or that senior leaders would reject their creative ideas.

- Videos I was unhappy with and therefore had to reject, or at a minimum recommend a completely different creative approach (yes, I see the irony related to the point above). The marketing team's fears are frequently legitimate.

- Videos being produced that I was happy with and that the marketing team was happy with, but that closely connected constituencies (like board members) didn't find effective and wouldn't support. It is, as you might guess, very hard to make videos that both 16-year-olds and 55-year-olds like.

It's easy to look at this frustrating list and armchair-quarterback how these situations could be avoided. Better management, better communication, better vision casting and creative briefings to ensure everyone was on the same page. Better segmentation, better cost controls, better hiring and coaching. Criticize the list all you like; I'm pretty good at criticism, too. But the fact remains that many times these lessons are painfully learned and only obvious after the fact.

Don't get me wrong; I'm not trying to be critical of my place of employment. I'd imagine that a stroll through any corner office in corporate America would produce similar comments and sorrows from marketing teams that have tried and failed to effectively get their companies up and running on YouTube. This is true of teams that have good management and good creative talent. There is undoubtedly good reason why each marketing team that is experiencing a "failure to launch" is in that situation.

Your First Step Toward a Marketing Plan

This book is written with the goal of untangling these complicated issues and making them simple. Your YouTube marketing plan should not be complicated. My goal is that after reading this book, you'll be able to quickly and easily diagnose and remedy the frequent ailments and get on track. Let's look at ways you can diagnose the biggest and most common problems and start on your marketing plan.

There Are Only Three Possible Uses for YouTube

I know; it sounds wrong, but it's true—there are only three possible uses for YouTube. Yep, just three. And if you don't approach your marketing plan with an eye toward managing each one of them, your marketing will suffer. So the first step in a professional YouTube marketing plan is to understand the three uses and how your marketing message needs to be presented through each one. You cannot choose one and ignore the other two and expect to be successful. It's like the analogy of the three-legged stool. It takes all three legs for the stool to be useful. What are the three?

1. **Video hosting.** To use on YouTube or on other sites as embedded videos

2. **Social networking**. To serve and connect with a target audience in a social way

3. **Paid advertising**. To spend advertising dollars to attract viewers or clicks

Your greatest gains on YouTube will occur when you take each of these aspects of the site and use them effectively in combination. You want your YouTube engine firing on all cylinders, and this is how you do it. When you use all three aspects together, you'll have a vibrant channel with a good number of views, subscribers, and comments. You'll see healthy growth in these areas, and you'll also see solid growth in the most important metric of all: the amount of traffic that comes from YouTube and goes to your website.

POWER TIP

Your first step toward a solid YouTube marketing plan is to understand the three uses of the site and prepare to operate in each one of them effectively.

The Most Common Mistake

When you see a company that has bad results on YouTube, you'll frequently find that the company is treating YouTube as a video-hosting site but completely ignoring the social networking and advertising aspects. It won't work out well. There are at least three reasons this is a bad idea:

1. Because if you're on YouTube, people will look at your profile and videos and ask one simple question, "Are these guys legit?" If you only have a few hundred followers and a few thousand video views, then you're providing a simple answer—no. This is true of your prospects, current customers, and even competitors.

2. Because your customers want to connect with you. They assume that if you're on YouTube, then you're doing it on a professional level. That means you are willing to engage with them socially.

3. Because your competitors can easily fulfill your customers' needs. If you don't engage socially on YouTube, then you are leaving a huge advantage wide open to your competitors. Likewise, if you never advertise on YouTube, you are leaving low-cost traffic on the table for them to pick up.

So to avoid the most common mistakes on YouTube, simply ask the question, are we using it for all three purposes, or are we just using it for hosting? If you just need a video-hosting platform, then you should choose another option.

The Second Most Common Mistake

There is another temptation for online marketers that emerges, which is simply to use YouTube for advertising purposes and not for hosting or social media. You can advertise to drive traffic to your website (and you should); we'll talk more about that in upcoming chapters. But if you only use it for advertising without any substantial presence on the site, then your first impression to prospective customers will be really bad. So if you have a pile of money waiting to be used on advertising and you want to use part of it on YouTube, then be sure to create some great video content, set up your channel for social success, and start using the advertising options. Your advertising dollars will go much farther and have a greater impact if you're presenting a fully mature marketing strategy.

Conclusions

Your YouTube marketing plan is ready to come together. In this chapter, we gave you the basic framework that you can begin to use to outline your work. In the next chapter, we'll look into the two reasons people will actually take the time to watch your videos. Before you can make videos that will work, you've got to know why people watch them. Let's dive into that next.

And Action!

(1) Begin to outline your YouTube marketing plan, focusing on the three functional areas of the site: video hosting, social networking, and advertising. (2) Determine if you're in a corporate climate that makes YouTube marketing difficult or if you're in an entrepreneurial setting that allows YouTube marketing to be simpler. If the latter, use it to your advantage to dominate your niche or industry when it comes to YouTube marketing. (3) Be sure to avoid the most common mistakes: using YouTube for video hosting alone or using it for advertising alone.

Part 2

GETTING
STARTED
SUCCESSFULLY

YouTube

There Are Only Two Reasons People Will Watch Your Video

know; it seems like an overly simple statement, but it's true. There are just two reasons people will watch your video. This actually holds true for any type of creative content you produce, whether it's writing a book, conducting a webinar, painting a picture, or putting on a seminar. So before we talk about effective video-creation strategies, we need to understand the reasons why someone would take the time to watch your video. As a next step in your marketing plan, you need to adapt these reasons to your niche or industry and ask the following question: How could these apply to your prospects?

The Two Reasons People Will Watch Your Video

Let's review the two reasons, and then we'll tackle the question of how you might apply this to your niche or industry situation.

Reason #1. Curiosity

The first reason people will watch a video is curiosity. We are curious by nature. We want to see what is about to happen. We want to have mysteries explained. We like the suspense created by interesting titles and taglines and want to get resolution. This chapter is a good example. I'm guessing that as soon as you read, "There are only two reasons people will watch your video," your curiosity was aroused. You wondered if it was true, you wondered what the two reasons were, you wondered if you already knew this information or if you had heard it before, and you wondered if you were going to agree or disagree with the information in this chapter. Wow—you are curious!

Watch Them Leave

People bring the same level of curiosity to watching videos. If you look at your YouTube analytics (we'll talk about those later), you can clearly see this phenomenon at work. Simply look at the data that tell you when people start leaving a certain video. You'll see the exact second that viewership starts to decline. When you look at the data, it's easy to ask the question whether you satisfied their curiosity and if as a result they are no longer engaged. Frequently the answer is yes. As soon as you satisfy people's curiosity, they will begin to exit the video.

This psychological phenomenon is one of the most powerful triggers you can use in your marketing efforts. You can make videos that ask an intriguing question or propose an interesting idea. That gets people in the door; then you simply spend the majority of the video unpacking the answer or revealing the how-to.

> **POWER TIP**
>
> If you know people leave your video when you've satisfied their curiosity, then don't satisfy their curiosity completely until the end of the video. You can even say, "Stick around to the end of the video because I'm going to reveal how . . ." Use your creativity to structure videos that keep people engaged to the end.

Reason #2. Motivated Self-Interest

This is a broader category. It includes a whole array of possible "reasons behind the reason." Although it's frequently difficult to fully understand people's motivations for watching videos, you can be sure that they are doing it to satisfy their self-interest, not yours. Their self-interest might include any one of the following (or a combination of them all at once):

■ **Learning something new.** People love to learn. And the Internet has been a gold mine of self-education. Frequently, a video is a better way to learn than finding a written explanation of something. The Khan Academy is a good example of a YouTube channel that is dedicated to teaching new things and facilitating learning. With over 2,200 videos and millions of video views, the channel is laser-beam-focused on this one simple goal.

■ **Laughing.** People love to laugh. And they'll laugh at the strangest things. Comedy comes in all shapes and sizes. And the best part of humorous videos is that people love to share them, rewatch them, and return to them for months or even years to come.

■ **Problem solving.** People love to solve problems themselves, and the invention of YouTube how-to videos has enabled countless stubborn do-it-yourselfers to get things done with just enough help to make them feel empowered. Some answers to hard problems are better demonstrated than explained in writing.

■ **Sentimentality or remembering.** People love to reminisce. In some ways, this is the history and origin of watching videos at home—in the old days, it was home movies or slide shows on the old carousel slide projectors. Now people can relive fun times and events with the videos hosted on YouTube.

■ **Entertainment.** People love to be entertained. And when you can make a boring topic entertaining, you've got a shot at attracting a huge following. Entertainment doesn't have to be over-the-top theatrical presentations. It can be as simple as having a nice location to shoot a video, a nice presence on camera, or a sense of humor when presenting.

■ **Winning.** People love to win. The fun comes not only from the tangible reward provided but also from the emotional reward they feel when they win. People will work hard to win. At Liberty Jane

Clothing, we've seen people do extraordinary video responses just for the chance to win one of our contests. You might be surprised how hard your prospects and current customers might work to win something from you.

- **Bonding.** People love to meet new people. And if you have a brand that they respect and enjoy, then they'll be honored to connect with you. It's a privilege to meet CEOs or "insiders" at the companies we revere. When people watch an "inside our office" video from a company they love, they bond more tightly with the brand. They move from customer to advocate.

- **Being discovered.** People want to be discovered. They want to be respected, known, and liked. When you create a context in which people get known, they are grateful for it. People appreciate the "stardom" that's made possible by winning contests and being a regular on your YouTube channel.

Always Capitalize on the Two Reasons

Your videos need to be created to appeal to one of the two reasons we've outlined in this chapter. Any topic, no matter how seemingly boring, can work if you create it to resonate with one of these reasons. If you want to find excellent examples, simply search for TED Talks on YouTube, and you'll find a huge number of videos that usually appeal to people's curiosity. The TED Talks videos do that through their titles—titles like:

- "Reach into the Computer and Grab a Pixel"

- "Is the Obesity Crisis Hiding a Bigger Problem?"

- "The Thrilling Potential of Sixth Sense Technology"

- "Arthur Benjamin Does Mathamagic"

But the TED Talks videos don't stop there. At the brand level, they've cultivated a reputation of being a terrific place to learn something new. So even when people don't have their curiosity piqued by the title of one of the videos, they give the video the benefit of the doubt and watch it because of the power of the brand.

Good Ways to Capitalize on the Two Reasons

So how do you make a video that will capitalize on one of these reasons? It's not difficult. You can do it in several ways. Let's review them.

Your UWP

Randomness doesn't draw a crowd on YouTube. It's just the opposite; consistency of videos draws a crowd. So the best way to build a loyal following is to make it very clear what you're all about and keep doing it for the long haul. This becomes your YouTube channel's *unique watching proposition*—let's call it your UWP. It's the answer to the question, why should I watch your videos? It's the brand attribute that people associate with your YouTube channel. It can be different from your brand's primary attributes. For example, your brand might be known as the ultrapremium luxury provider in your niche or industry. But your YouTube channel can be known for having hilarious videos. Or maybe your brand is well known for being the low-cost provider in your niche. But your YouTube channel can become known for making incredibly good educational videos.

Decide up front what your YouTube channel is going to be about and stick with it. Is it education? Is it comedy? Is it entertainment? I know what you're thinking—it's about selling my products! But it's got to be more sophisticated than that. You've got to decide how you're going to help people meet their needs, and at the same time you need to build a platform that allows you to share details about your products, your company, and your special promotions and sales.

You do this by developing a primary video approach and perfecting it. Then, when it makes sense, create additional videos that simultaneously both meet people's needs and accomplish your business objectives. Let's look at a few examples:

- You can have a YouTube channel that primarily offers comedy videos, but occasionally you make a serious video about an educational topic and give a heartfelt presentation about something you care about.

- You can have a teaching channel that shows people how to do interesting projects, but then occasionally you run a contest to promote one of your new products.

- You can have a product review channel that explains the pros and cons of new products in your niche or industry, but then occasionally you make a funny rap video (if that's what you're good at).

When you get really good at your primary video style, then weave in an alternative style to get people bonding with you in a powerful way. People feel like you're revealing more of your personality, and they appreciate it. Treat your primary video style like your meat and potatoes and your alternative style like the special treat.

Your Title

The title of your video is the first and most important positioning tool at the individual video level. Make it work hard for you. Think about the curiosity and motivated self-interest inherent within your industry or niche and create titles that will resonate with your prospects.

Your Opening Sentence

The most common way to let people know what they're in for if they watch your video is to simply script it so that in the first three seconds you tell people right up front what it's going to be about. Statements like these are very common and effective:

- "Hi everybody, in this video I'm going to show you how to make a . . ."

- "Let's talk about . . ."

- "Have you ever wondered . . ."

Your Video's Still Image

YouTube will take two screenshots of your video when it is uploaded, and one of those screenshots will be the image available for your video. So when people run across your video, that screenshot is what they'll see. You can manage this to your advantage if you know when the screenshots will be taken. You simply put your best or most interesting images in the right spots in your video. The YouTube screenshots occur at one-third and three-quarters of the way through your video. So count the minutes and seconds and work to put your best-looking clips in those spots.

Your Video Description

You have the opportunity to describe your video in the description field. You should do your best copywriting here. Spend the time to write compelling copy and give people a good reason to watch the whole video. Tell them what you've got in store for them and make it interesting.

Effective Video Styles That Resonate with the Two Reasons

You don't need to reinvent the wheel when it comes to video creation. There are dozens of effective video styles that you can replicate and adapt to your situation. Part of this will depend on your personality, which we'll talk about in the next chapter. But part of it can simply be a calculated decision about how best to serve your prospects. Let's review some of the most commonly used video styles.

The How-to Video

Of all the video formats, the how-to video is probably the most effective on YouTube. Ask yourself how it can be applied to your niche or industry. If your competitors are already using it, ask yourself how you can create a how-to video with a different spin.

The Product Demonstration Video

Interesting and creative product demonstrations are a great tool on YouTube. But if they are boring or predictable, they will be avoided. One of the best strategies is to get other people to do a product demonstration for your products, and then you can feature them. That allows you to benefit from third-party endorsements.

The Mastery Demonstration Video

A terrific video format is to demonstrate mastery of something. People will watch a master at work in almost any niche or industry. This is true of video game players, musicians, and performers of all kinds. If you have a difficult-to-master product, then make videos of people mastering it.

The Product Wow Video

Some product videos are impressive because they show off what a product can do in an amazing way. The Blendtec folks used this style to perfection when they created their *Will It Blend?* videos. Who wouldn't want to watch an iPhone being blended?

The Watch Me Try It Video

People love to watch other people fail. If your niche or industry has a hard action or activity that takes a lot of mastery, then you can make videos where you show your failures. These videos fall somewhere between comedy and education, and people love watching them.

The My Version Video

A tremendously popular video style is the "cover" video approach. Doing a song, dance, or other performing art with your own style and approach is fun for people to watch.

The Funny Slice-of-Life Video

Sometimes life is funny. *Case in point:* The *Charlie Bit My Finger* video is the most watched video of all time on YouTube. The video simply shows an older brother playing with his younger brother, Charlie, until things turn serious and Charlie bites his brother's finger. Are there slice-of-life videos that can be funny in your niche or industry?

The Comedy Show Video

There are thousands of aspiring comedians out there, and they've discovered that they can take their acts straight to the people via YouTube. The Rhett & Link videos are good examples. Their *Good Mythical Morning* show is wildly popular and has made them Internet celebrities. Can you leverage this video format to your business, niche, or industry? Maybe you're not funny, but you have staff members who are. Or maybe you should just identify a local comedian who would be willing to work with you to promote your products.

The Screen-Capture Teaching Video

An educational format that works very well is the screen-capture video. You can create this kind of video by using one of many types of screen-capture software. With it, you can show how to do anything on your computer—from tutorials to video game run-throughs. If your niche or industry has any type of associated software or online process, then you have an opportunity to create a screen-capture video. Maybe it's as simple as making a screen-capture video as part of your customer service efforts that shows people how to navigate your website and use your services.

The Outrageous Behavior Video

The popularity of the Jackass brand cannot be ignored. People love watching other people do something outrageous, risky, or dangerous. The popular X Games provide a good example of this video format. If your product has an element of danger or risk, think about how you can create videos that show off that aspect.

The Harlem Shake Video

Have you heard of the Harlem Shake? It is a dance video style that went viral and produced an amazing online phenomenon. Companies, individuals, schools, churches, and community groups all produced their own video versions of this dance. The point was to simply have fun. That was it. This phenomenon has run its course, so I wouldn't recommend doing one now, but I would suggest that you pay attention to these types of social trends and, when the time is right, jump on the bandwagon.

And Action!

(1) Consider how the two reasons play out in your niche or industry and how your company can use them. (2) Decide on a primary video style that will become your UWP. (3) Choose a primary video style and learn how to do it better than your competition. (4) Choose a secondary video style and learn how to supplement your primary style with it.

Chapter 5

Defining Your Style

I n this chapter, we're going to discuss you and the role you play on YouTube. Don't worry; we'll get you on-screen in a way that works for you—and a way that also positions you well with your target audience. Of all the hurdles to effective YouTube marketing, getting the on-screen talent aspects figured out is probably the hardest assignment. Get it right, and the video views and subscriber growth will happen. Get it wrong, and your YouTube marketing efforts will stall.

Our Challenges at Liberty Jane Clothing

On February 13, 2008, we launched our first contest video on YouTube. It got over 7,000 video views and dozens of entries (video responses). (We'll talk more about contests in upcoming chapters and explain how to do this type of video.) Before that first contest, we had only done videos that showed our products with a music soundtrack. We inserted those simpler product videos into our eBay auction listings. They were just still photos in a slide-show format set to music. That was working well to help us sell our products on eBay, but we wanted to do more on YouTube. We wanted a way to attract a bigger following and give something back to our new community of followers. We thought a contest video would be a fun way to engage a crowd.

We knew this contest video had to be different from our prior videos. It would be the first video where we had an on-screen presence. Someone had to explain the rules and share the details. There was no way around it; someone was going to have to step in front of the camera. This was when we hit our first roadblock to YouTube success.

Here is our little secret: my wife and our head designer, Cinnamon, is the logical person to have on camera, but the truth is, she doesn't enjoy it much. It stresses her out. She'll do it, but she won't volunteer for the assignment. And since I have a face for radio and I didn't want to be known as the "creepy guy on YouTube doing doll clothes design contests," we had a real problem. We had a talent problem.

Our solution was pretty simple. At the time, our youngest daughter, Liberty Jane, was just five and a complete show-off. She was in dance and loved to be on camera. She was naturally confident and outgoing, and she not only had a cute look but also had a very funny personality. We had found our primary "spokesgirl." The video-creation process was pretty simple. I'd explain to her what we were doing and then give her lines to repeat in small chunks. She'd repeat them after me as the camera rolled, and then later I would edit her sections together so it was a seamless presentation of the content. You can see in Figure 5.1 what this looked like.

Figure 5.1 Here is Liberty's first on-camera role to announce our first contest.

Fast-forward to the spring of 2013. We had done over 250 videos, including several contests each year for five years. We had grown into the routine of Libby playing the spokesgirl role in exchange for $10 for each video. Hey, some videos only take 10 minutes to make, so it's not bad money for a kid. As you might guess, in the five years, our little girl had grown up! And the truth was that by the spring of 2013, her interest in making videos had declined a lot as her personality matured. She was now a young woman and the type of role she had played in 2005 wasn't the same role she could play in 2013 (see Figure 5.2). We needed to come up with a new video style that would work.

Figure 5.2 Our spokesgirl grew up over the course of five years.

Our second-generation video work put Cinnamon back in the spotlight. But as you might guess, she still hadn't grown too much enthusiasm for being on-screen. So we needed to find a video format that would work well for her personality. We found it in the "slightly off-screen" approach that is very popular with the how-to and DIY type of videos. Cinnamon has found that if she's speaking and showing something, she's more comfortable than if she's front and center on the screen (see Figure 5.3).

Figure 5.3 Cinnamon would rather be slightly off-screen and primarily have a speaking role.

The On-Screen Persona

Obviously, Liberty's on-screen persona was young, cute, and happy. Cinnamon's on-screen persona is friendly, knowledgeable, and instructive. The idea of the "on-screen persona" or "archetypal role" is critical for you to understand in order to establish a trusted personality that will click with people on YouTube. I know; you didn't expect us to talk about psychology in a book about YouTube marketing, but it has a huge part to play, and it can be your marketing secret weapon.

The concept of the archetypal role goes back to psychiatrist Carl Jung, who described it in his book *Structure of the Psyche*. He believed that archetypes are models of people, behaviors, or personalities. These models are well known to all of us. They are behaviors and personalities that we immediately recognize and are familiar with, even if a new person is playing the part. It's like a new actor playing the part of Batman. You still know that Batman is going to do Batman stuff, even if Val Kilmer is out and Christian Bale is in. Your mind permits the change in actor and clings to the archetypal role or character attributes.

Growing up, most of us watched hours of TV every day, and in the process we have been exposed to these types of on-screen roles our entire lives. We know them very well. They are hardwired into our brains. They are imprinted onto us. We are comfortable with them and accept them. Take a stroll through YouTube and see if you can't begin to identify common archetypes or personas. Once your eyes are opened to this aspect of the site, you'll see those archetypes everywhere.

How do you get new prospects to discover you and instantly bond with you on YouTube? How do you make these prospects immediately comfortable with you, your brand, and your products and messages? It's simple, really. You play a role that they are already familiar with and will understand subconsciously almost instantaneously. Your on-screen persona is your trick to get past all the usual buyer defenses. They will immediately click with you if they recognize the on-screen persona you are playing. At an emotional or even subconscious level, they will "get" you. It turns out there are shortcuts to trust.

> **POWER TIP**
>
> Pick an on-screen persona and stay true to it. Take it as your role to play and don't deviate. Your prospects and customers will bond with you as you play a part they are already familiar with and trust.

Common On-Screen Personas

There are a number of on-screen personas available to choose from. Our society has reinforced and embellished many of them to the point where they are very well known and highly trusted. Let's review them, and as we do, see if you can identify popular figures in our society who fit into these roles.

The Expert

The expert is one of the most common roles to play. It is created by having authority on a topic and is supported by credibility indicators that people trust and respect. Do you have a PhD? Have you written a best-selling book on the topic? Do you teach at a university? Have you proved yourself to be successful in the field? All these attributes are helpful credibility indicators that establish you as an expert. But many times, credibility is assumed when your video presentation style is excellent. Conversely, if your video presentation style is poor, no one will believe you're an expert.

The Nerd

The nerd role is a twist on the expert persona. It is a style that focuses on geekiness and technology expertise. Nerds can be clueless about social skills but almost godlike when it comes to technology.

The Wunderkind

The German word *wunderkind* means "wonder child" and refers to a child prodigy. This type of child has incredible skill at a very early age. Silicon Valley has a long history of searching for and idolizing these types of kids. Steve Jobs was in this role early on. Mark Zuckerberg has been more recently. It would seem that Justin Bieber benefited from falling into this category when his mom put up his first YouTube video.

The Sage

The sage persona is typified by wisdom. A sage is a wise person who has learned to apply knowledge of a certain issue to life. Sages are experts who focus more on application and coaching than on technical skills. They teach the truths that they have learned in a trusting and caring way.

The Genius

The genius is an expert or savant who has complete mastery of his or her topic, along with the attributes of a superior intellect. The TED Talks seem to position their speakers, almost without trying, as geniuses. You get the impression that every TED speaker is smarter than the average person.

The Average Guy

The average guy persona is an unassuming, friendly role. It is the role that most smart salespeople try to portray. The best-known average guy personality in recent years was Tim Taylor's sidekick, Al Borland, on the hit TV show *Home Improvement*. Tim played the jester, and Al played the average guy. You may have noticed that Richard Karn, the actor who played Al Borland, is still using that persona effectively in TV commercials.

The Trainer

There is a difference between an expert, a sage, and a trainer. A trainer focuses on showing you how to do something. Trainer personas can do very well in many skill areas, including knitting and sewing, photography, drawing, yoga and exercise, dog training, guitar playing, and gardening. The persona can be used in any situation in which show-and-tell videos are helpful.

The Creator

This persona is best used in the artisan fields. When we decided to have Cinnamon be on camera for Liberty Jane Clothing, we positioned her as a creator-expert. We've worked to reinforce that combination archetype throughout our marketing efforts, so that it becomes associated with her online personality. Creators can gather huge followers on YouTube in niche areas. In Chapter 9, we'll meet the team members at My Froggy Stuff and look at their work, which has 111 million video views as of this writing.

The Jester

The jester persona is a comedian archetype. Jesters are great at making people laugh (see Figure 5.4). They use physical comedy as well as jokes and skits to share their funny views of the world. YouTube has proved to be incredibly valuable to up-and-coming comedians. They've realized that they can attract their own audiences and gain huge exposure by building a YouTube followership of their own. This leads to additional opportunities. It also leads to a nice revenue stream as their videos are watched over and over.

Figure 5.4 Rhett & Link have built a thriving online audience with their comedy channels.

The Innocent (or Child)

The innocent is the archetype of purity, innocence, and childhood. This is the archetype that Liberty fell into when she became our spokesgirl.

The Explorer

The explorer persona is focused on being a rugged individualist. In the last few years, the TV personality Bear Grylls played this role perfectly in the adventure series *Man vs. Wild*.

Close Up with Rhett & Link

Rhett McLaughlin and Link Neal have created a thriving comedy channel on YouTube, with over 1.2 million followers on their primary channel and over 500,000 subscribers on their secondary channel. Between the two channels, they've accumulated more than 260 million video views. We asked them to share some of their story with us and tell us how they've approached YouTube to build a thriving business.

▪ Q. When and how did you first envision using YouTube for business?

A. In 2007, after having our YouTube channel for about a year, we began cold-calling small companies. We'd have an idea and then call a phone number on a website and attempt to talk the owner into paying us to feature their brand in one of our videos. After many phone calls, we were able to talk AJJCornhole.com into sponsoring our "Cornhole Song" and iResQ.com into sponsoring our "Dead iPod Song." At that moment, we thought we might have a business model.

▪ Q. What specific steps have you taken to boost your YouTube results?

A. Our most consistent strategy has been to make very shareable content. We try to make videos that start a conversation and result in a new viewer. On a very practical level, we are students of the way YouTube works. We've learned that there is a lot of power in a good title and thumbnail. So, after making sure to create quality content, we attempt to package it as well as we can.

▪ Q. What were some of the early challenges or struggles you faced?

A. Very early on, our main challenge was building an audience that could support a career. Even after being on YouTube for two years, our goal was to consistently get 10,000 views on our videos. We never had one blockbuster video that single-handedly built our audience. It was a slow process.

Q. How did you overcome that?

A. We just kept making videos. We tried to learn as much as we could from audience feedback and continued teaching ourselves video making. The timing worked out very well for us. Just as we were figuring things out, YouTube was becoming a mainstream source of entertainment. When people showed up, we were there with a video catalog for them to see. By 2009, we had gained the critical mass needed for a sustainable career in online video.

Q. What "aha" moments have you experienced where you realized you could do something differently or better to boost your YouTube results?

A. In the early days, we discovered that you have to take people's expectations about online video into account. We released our "Facebook Song" within a 10-minute podcast format, and it got a few thousand views. Later, we released it on its own as a music video, and it started amassing huge numbers of views. Today it has over 13 million.

Q. What results or successes have you achieved because of YouTube?

A. In addition to forming a growing production company based on our videos, almost everything we've worked on in the past five years has been a result of our YouTube presence. Our first TV hosting opportunity, our TV show, our commercial directing, and producing videos outside of our channel—it's all a result of people seeing our YouTube videos.

Q. If you were sitting down with someone just getting started with YouTube, what advice would you give?

A. It's such a different environment than when we first got started. It's much tougher to build an audience. At the same time, there are so many people on YouTube now, that the potential for audience building is greater than ever. Our advice would be to do something specific, consistent, and excellent. If your content is something that's never been done before for an audience that doesn't have an existing source of web videos, even better.

And Action!

(1) Consider which personas will work for your audience and how you might use one or more of them. (2) Evaluate your own personal strengths and style and determine which persona you'd be comfortable playing. (3) Begin planning how your approach to YouTube can use both a specific style of video and a specific persona. (4) Take Rhett & Link's advice and start doing something specific, consistent, and excellent.

Seven Ways to Get Your Videos Done

The previous chapters have explained the benefits of YouTube marketing, the challenges businesses face, and the strategic approaches necessary for success. Now it's time to make some awesome videos. In this chapter, we'll walk through seven no-hassle methods for getting your video production off to a great start.

The System Is the Solution

Before we outline specific video production strategies, we need to talk about the high-level goal here. Remember that old AT&T slogan, "The system is the solution"? When it comes to video production work, you want to think in terms of building a system of video production, not simply creating one video. Creating one video won't attract a faithful following. Creating one video won't produce tons of traffic, unless you get insanely lucky. Creating one video won't explain to viewers what you're all about. One-video-at-a-time thinking is just unwise. But with a pipeline of successful videos, you build continuity that is incredibly helpful.

Imagine a new pastor coming into a town and preaching one sermon. Will that one sermon build a huge following? No. But if that pastor is insanely good at preaching, then it won't take too long for the word to spread and people to begin to show up. Soon, a huge new church will form. You're in the same situation on YouTube. Your channel is your church. Your video is your sermon. Begin to think about a series of 10 or 20 videos and about the system necessary to create them.

1. The Cheapest Way to Get Your Videos Done

The best possible way to get your first few videos done is to do them yourself. Granted, it's probably the most stressful way if you're not familiar with video production work. But you'll learn the process. You'll learn what software is involved and how to use it, and you'll learn the YouTube publishing process. Of course, this is also the cheapest possible way to get videos completed.

Some people won't have any hesitation with this recommendation. In fact, they'd prefer to do it all. Sometimes control freaks make the best artistic products. So if you are game to shoot your own videos, go for it. As with learning any new trade skill, the learning curve at the beginning is going to be very painful. But once you master the basic skills, the process becomes much easier.

The other clear advantage of doing it yourself is the in-depth knowledge you'll have when you do decide to subcontract it out later. If you've done it yourself, you cannot be conned into overpaying. When you've done it yourself, you can call "BS" when a video producer tells you that something can't be done or that doing something is "really expensive." You will not be played for a fool by unscrupulous videographers. For that reason alone, it is probably wise to make a few of your first videos.

In upcoming chapters, we'll walk through the actual video-creation process so you have all the information you need to start your project and finish it with a solid video that you can be proud of. Don't worry; a good video is easier to make than you might think.

2. Someone on Your Team

Another simple way to get video production work under way is to assign it to someone on your team. Depending on the size of your business, it might not be too difficult to assign the video production work to someone who has the inclination to do it. It wouldn't be surprising if that person was young, artistic, and tech savvy.

The easiest way to find someone on your team to pick up the ball and run with it is to inquire broadly and ask if anyone has a passion for videography and a willingness to start making it happen. If training is needed, then investing in one of your existing team members is a much better use of funds than paying a contractor for a one-time video project.

Of course, this would put you in the role of the executive producer—not directing the video, but approving it and backing it financially. Being an executive producer is much harder than directing a video, since you have to communicate your wishes through another layer of management. You have to trust that the person making the video shares your vision for it, understands your point of view, and has the talent to create a good finished product.

3. The Friends and Family Approach

An alternative way to get video production accomplished is to include friends or family members who might have a knack for the work and are willing to work for free. As you might guess, tons of teenagers are incredibly competent with a video camera and the editing software needed. Is one of them your niece or nephew?

The friends and family approach can be a great way to go if you have the time and patience to coordinate their involvement. Their commitment to the project will only be as strong as their commitment to you.

The downside of the friends and family approach is that they're not being paid. They can walk out on you without a moment's notice. Additionally, if they aren't doing a good job, you may find it difficult to remove them from the project.

4. The College Connection

In most metropolitan areas or college towns, video courses are offered at local schools. Look through the college directory and find the professor responsible for teaching video production, usually as part of the communications department. Professors in these classes are great talent scouts and can act as a matchmaker between you and gifted students.

The best part about using college kids is that they're eager to find work, eager to please, and early enough in their careers to not be too expensive. Who knows; maybe your video work can be part of a classroom assignment and not require any budget at all.

Most college students who are good enough to make a quality video are already taking on clients and doing semiprofessional projects, so they'll know how to work with you. They will also have a good understanding of what is hip and contemporary.

The downside of using college students is that they will probably be less familiar with your niche or industry than you'd prefer. They might not have any familiarity with your product line either, but these are short-term problems. You might need to provide an orientation or training on what your company is all about.

5. Interns

If you find a good video maker at the local college, then a fantastic next step is available. Offer the student an internship as your videographer. You can lock in the relationship for a semester or more. You provide the student with education and insight into your business, and he or she creates great videos—a match made in heaven.

The downside of using interns is that an increasing amount of regulation is entering this area, which means you need to check to ensure you are complying with all local, state, and federal requirements. You don't want to use interns for free labor, so there truly needs to be an educational benefit that they receive.

Of course, if you can have one video intern, why not three or four? Your ability to create a pipeline of videos is amplified if you can find more talent to manage. Chances are good that your intern team can produce a tremendous amount of video content and maybe manage the social media aspects of YouTube as well.

6. The Contract Gig

When your less expensive options have been exhausted, you can always turn to finding a videographer available for hire. There are a remarkable number of contract videographers ready, willing, and able to make you a fantastic video.

There are lots of websites that offer listings of videographers. You might try, for example, Videographies.com, GigSalad.com, or Fiverr .com. Each of these sites lists freelancers who are currently looking for clients. Fiverr in particular is interesting, as the work is generally $5. Can you get an amazing product video for $5? No, probably not. But there is a surprisingly large list of video projects on Fiverr. You can get things like professional intros (the initial few seconds of a video) or product testimonials.

Our personal experience with Fiverr has been great. We regularly hire the same contractors to do special projects for us that we cannot easily do ourselves. After finding a good contractor for a specific type of work, there is no reason to continue shopping around. The person gets to know you, and you get to know the person. It's a great way to build a relationship with a freelancer whom you wouldn't otherwise ever meet.

If there are aspects of your video production work that seem like a challenge, look to see if there is a Fiverr freelancer who is willing to do it for you. The "Video & Animation" section on Fiverr includes gigs in the following categories:

- "Commercials"

- "Editing & Post Production"

- "Animation & 3D"

- "Testimonials & Reviews by Actors"

- "Puppets"

- "Stop Motion"

- "Intros"

You might be wondering why people would work for $5. The truth is, there are gigs on Fiverr that cost more than $5, and frequently the total cost of a transaction can be much higher. Additionally, some of the people on Fiverr do $5 gigs as a way to find new prospective clients. They use it as a lead-generation source for their businesses. When you think about it, that's pretty smart. Instead of marketing and paying for leads, they're getting leads and a small amount of money as well. So don't assume that the level of quality on Fiverr is necessarily bad. Sometimes it is remarkably good. We are frequently pleasantly surprised.

> **POWER TIP**
> Fiverr.com has professional videographers waiting to work with you. Why would they do video work for $5? They are looking for new clients whom they can build long-term relationships with. It's a win-win solution.

One way to ensure you get a good experience on Fiverr and similar sites is to search for freelancers who have very high ratings on the site. On different sites, a high rating is called different things. On Fiverr, it's designated as a "Top Rated Seller." It's easy to find on Fiverr; simply search by rating. So in any category, such as "Video & Animation," you can search by rating, and the Top Rated Sellers will be listed first. Frequently, we look for people with good ratings but not the highest ratings. Why? Often, the highest-rated freelancers can be overwhelmed with work and are sometimes victims of their own success, with slower delivery times and less overall creativity.

7. The Barter Partner

Do you have a business skill that can be used to barter with a videographer? Maybe you're a marketer, CPA, or copywriter, and a videographer is actively searching for your skills and talents right now. Barter for services.

There are various ways to go about finding these types of options. One of the largest online sites is International Monetary Systems. You can find it online at http://www.imsbarter.com. The network has over 16,000 member businesses, including video production companies. If you have goods or services that could be valuable to other companies, then this is an option to consider.

According to *Bloomberg Businessweek*, the U.S. barter market is an amazing $12 billion industry. You can learn more about this vast world at the International Reciprocal Trade Association (http://www.irta .com). Your participation in a professional association of this type could benefit your business in many other ways beyond just videography.

Another simple way to find a barter partner is through your local chamber of commerce or community groups like Rotary Clubs. Locally networking to find a good partner is hard work, but if you find a good prospective partner, you could develop a business relationship that lasts for many years.

Three Setups

In a recent Freedom Ocean podcast, Tim Reid, Australia's number one marketing podcaster, interviewed James Schramko about his videorecording setups. James described three setups that are useful for us to understand. I asked James if I could share part of his interview, and he graciously agreed. You can learn more about Tim at http://www .smallbusinessbigmarketing.com and about James at http://www.super fastbusiness.com. To hear the entire interview, visit http://www .freedomocean.com and look for episode #60. Let's jump into their conversation:

> **Tim:** What I've observed by those who are creating ongoing videos is they have a wonderful setup where they simply sit down and push "record." How do you get to that point? What do you need?
>
> **James:** Yep, so you've got three main elements here. You've got sound, the camera, and the lighting. They're the three things you've got to consider.
>
> ### An Easy Setup
>
> **James:** The easy setup is I've got my Rode Podcaster plugged into the computer and my Logitech C920 camera. That just sits on the screen. So that camera and microphone setup will give a really good-quality sound and a good-quality picture.
>
> And then in terms of lighting, I'm actually using natural light straight through the window, which is a bit dodgy, because it can fluctuate. So ideally, you'll have a consistent light, so like a three-light setup. Your main light, your key light, and your backlight to give that contrast.
>
> ### A More Professional Setup
>
> **James:** My more professional setup is a Canon DSLR camera; it's a 60D, and I use a Rode Shotgun mic for that. It plugs into the camera.

And when I want to set up, I literally turn on the lights. I have it in the same spot, the same setup. So all I have to do is turn the camera on, the lights on, and the microphone on, and I'm filming. When I'm finished, I take the SD card and plug it into my computer, and I now have high-quality video and audio in one track.

The Out-and-About Setup

James: Now, the third setup I have is when I'm out and about. I will use an iPad Mini and a [Samson] Zoom H4 microphone. And the Zoom H4 will give me great quality sound. Far better than you can get from the iPad Mini itself. And the iPad Mini will give me full HD, and I can then use an app called TiltShift Video, which gets me the ability to blur and smooth and adjust contrast and render it as if it's like a DSLR effect.

Tim: So for the easy setup, you're going to have an audio file and a video file. So how do you match those up?

James: ScreenFlow. I love ScreenFlow. You go to ScreenFlow preferences, and you select this camera and that mic. And it will bring in the audio and will match the video.

Tim: Let's talk more about the use of the iPad Mini. It has the same camera as your iPhone 5, so what's the advantage?

James: It has much better sound. So if most people don't have a Zoom, and most people won't, the iPad Mini has much better sound than the iPhone, in my experience.

It's much easier for a camera person to hold it, because it's easier to grab and hold stable. It gives you a much bigger display if you're filming yourself, and also the cover on it is quite handy. You can basically mount it on a desk or a windowsill, which I quite often do.

My best hack is I mount it on a windowsill, so I'm using natural light through the window, and I get really good light with that setup. The other hack I use is I put the cover over the [monitor] display, and I piggyback the iPad Mini on the laptop; and then I can put my Evernote right beside the camera lens, and it literally looks like I'm staring into the camera when I'm actually reading my Evernote prompt.

Tim: So in this setup you use your Zoom H4 for the audio, right? How do you synchronize your audio and video?

James: I plug the iPad Mini into the computer, and it synchronizes and I drag it into ScreenFlow. Then I drag in the .WAV file from the Zoom, which is the high-quality audio. And then I match up the signature of the audio, so it's synchronized.

Tim: That would be your #1 if you strip it all back?

James: So if you just had an iPad Mini, that would get you good enough quality video and sound to be in business. If you could only have one thing, that's probably the device you would need. And if you could have two devices, it would be the Zoom H4.

Tim: Thanks, James!

And Action!

(1) Identify your internal resistance to making videos and consider possible solutions. (2) Determine if you can create some of your first videos yourself so that you understand the process and learn the ropes. (3) Consider the pipeline of video production and how to keep the flow of new videos constantly going. (4) Consider using volunteers, students, or interns to accomplish your video production work. (5) Explore how sites like Fiverr.com can provide needed services inexpensively.

Partnering with Vloggers

n this chapter, we discuss the alternative video advertising approach known as experiential marketing. This form of advertising invites YouTube content creators and their audiences to have an up-close and personal experience with your product or brand. We'll do a close-up with a massive charity, World Vision Australia, and see how it teamed up with vloggers (video bloggers) by taking them all the way to rural Zambia to witness the transformation of communities working to bring themselves out of poverty. We'll see how that vlogging experience impacted the vloggers, their audiences, and the charity.

Instead of writing this chapter myself, I asked Richenda Vermuelen, the social media marketer who helped put together the World Vision Zambia vlogger program, to write about her experiences working on the project. She graciously agreed to help write the chapter. So without further ado, here's Richenda . . .

What Is a Vlog?

Already you might be wondering, What is a vlog? What is a vlogger? Let's break it down. The word *vlog* is a portmanteau of the words *video* and *blog*. And *vloggers* are people who create vlogs. That is to say, vloggers create videos of themselves discussing things and upload the videos to YouTube, where viewers can leave comments, give the thumbs up (or thumbs down), or even subscribe for future updates. Vlogs are just like blog posts, but they come in video format and can be thought of as a kind of Internet television.

While most people know about blogs, vlogging remains surprisingly unknown. It is a common myth that the only people posting videos of themselves online are lonely teens who are cooped up in their bedrooms, glued to laptops, reaching out to the Internet for a sense of human connection. This is not the case at all. Generally, vloggers make videos because they want to share their passions and interests with the world. Online communities flourish around vlogging, and you can bet that for any topic under the sun, there is a vlogger making videos about it and reaching out to an online community.

> **POWER TIP**
>
> The vlog audience consists largely of teenagers and young adults. Popular vlog genres include the following: film and entertainment, comedy, health and beauty, gaming, science and education, people and blogs, and pets and animals.

Some vloggers are extremely entertaining and attract an enormous amount of traffic to their videos. The most popular vloggers receive hundreds of thousands and even millions of views. For vloggers with such enormous online audiences, monetizing has made it possible for vlogging to become a viable career. Furthermore, their influence is similar to that of a celebrity. Vloggers whose videos manage to garner tens of thousands of views are still considered to be highly influential but are not quite held up to elite status, as they place more emphasis on the community aspect of vlogging. As for vloggers who only receive thousands or maybe even hundreds of views, emphasis is placed entirely on getting involved in the online community, rather than being an online influencer.

Experiential Marketing: A Form of Alternative Advertising

Experiential marketing is a cutting-edge way of engaging vloggers with your brand. Vloggers are far more likely to get on board with your product if you really offer them a unique experience, something out of the ordinary that goes beyond mere product placement. Something that really shows an understanding and appreciation for vloggers' influence and skills as communicators. Sometimes offering financial incentive doesn't work; vloggers might not have any interest in making money if it's at the expense of their integrity. Sometimes offering no-strings-attached gifts for product placement won't work either, because the vlogger might not connect with the product enough to make a video including it. This is when offering a vlogger a unique experience really stands out as something special and different.

What Does Experiential Marketing Look Like?

Vloggers shared some thoughts with us on experiential marketing:

> A motorbike company might say, "Do you want free motorbike lessons? We'll give you this new motorbike and you can make videos about it!" And it's tricky, because no matter how removed it is from your life and your interests, you always consider it. At first I think, *Maybe I do want motorbike lessons*. When you're offered a free experience, it's harder to turn down. I work with a major film company quite a lot. They are really great because they give you an experience, and if I like that experience, then I make a video about it. But they don't expect anything in return, so if I went to a new movie screening and didn't like the movie, I don't have to make a video about it. (Alex Day, *nerimon*)

> [Experiential marketing] has been the only thing I've actually done on YouTube that has tied in with brands. Vloggers can be really hard to corral! (Tom McLean, *frezned*)

Experiential marketing is different because it invites the vlogger to enjoy an intimate view of your brand. It is a form of alternative advertising that seeks to foster a relationship with the content creator, providing a meaningful experience that will translate into a compelling story that can be expressed via video. This element of story is key, as vloggers are professional storytellers. Successful experiential marketing endeavors are tailored to align with the interests and values of the vlogger.

Through correlating with the interests and values of the vlogger, this mode of advertising is socially elevated as a more authentic communication between the brand, the vlogger, and their larger audience. For this reason, the impact of experiential marketing upon vloggers and their audiences is often far more significant than other forms of advertising.

Experiential marketing is all about taking vloggers and their audiences on a journey, a journey that ties in with your brand in a meaningful way. It looks different depending on your brand. It might mean bringing your vlogger into the factory to get up close and personal with the sophisticated production of your product. It might mean inviting your vlogger into the studio to witness the generation of your media and converse openly with the skilled staff that makes it happen. It might mean inviting your vlogger to join your team at an international conference, with all-areas-access privileges. And it also means keeping with the values of taking care of your vlogger and giving him or her a no-strings-attached kind of experience, as this always serves to authenticate a brand-vlogger-audience interaction. You want your brand and the experience it is offering to be such that your vlogger will be compelled to share it.

Experiential marketing invites you and your team to think hard about your brand, to think what your brand means to people and what your brand *can* mean to people. Experiential marketing can realize the potential for your brand and your product to represent what you envision for it. It is a powerful tool that can transform the ways that people think about your brand.

World Vision Vloggers: An Experiential Marketing Case Study

In 2010, I was the social media manager of World Vision Australia, Australia's largest international relief and development charity. One of our greatest challenges was explaining the impact of World Vision's work. Poverty alleviation is complex, and World Vision's work has been largely misunderstood over the last four decades. However, we knew that there was a new generation of donors eager for more involvement, and we thought that partnering with YouTube celebrities could offer something brand new and exciting: a direct window into the reality of World Vision's work.

We invited Alex Day (*nerimon*, United Kingdom), Shawna Howson (*nanalew*, Canada), and Tom McLean (*frezned*, Australia) on a trip to Zambia to witness the fight against poverty firsthand. Why these three? We first looked in our backyard and found Tom, who had a large following (500,000 subscribers), a picture of his World Vision–sponsored child in one of his videos, and a knack for comedic commentary on the status quo. We learned that Tom had been sponsoring for over a decade and loved the idea of the communicative challenge. Tom introduced us to two of his friends, Shawna (100,000 subscribers) and Alex (250,000 subscribers), whom we quickly found to be a great fit. Shawna was compelling as someone who spoke from the heart in her videos, while Alex impressed us with his easy-to-understand narratives. All three storytellers had a unique style and diverse international audience, which we later learned was a winning combination.

What happened next was the most important element of the campaign. The four of us had a phone conversation about World Vision's challenges and the opportunity to see the work in action. The three vloggers offered creative ideas on how to make this campaign work. They owned the video execution and strategized ways to engage their audience. The "marketer" in me stepped down and made way for the "experience coordinator."

In Zambia, the vloggers were able to witness through their own eyes the actual process of communities bringing themselves out of poverty. It was amazing to see the communities flourish in this environment. As Shawna, Tom, and Alex captured large amounts of video footage and interacted with Zambian locals, I could see they were inspired to tell a better story. The vloggers each made a series of videos in which they shared the stories of the people they met and how World Vision affected people's lives. It all came together to create a beautiful, compelling picture of World Vision's work. And the initial talents I noticed came alive and captured the hearts and minds of their audiences. The vloggers were able to blend humor, wit, and compassion to keep their audiences engaged in poverty alleviation.

Some Comments from Viewers

"Hey, just wanted you to know that thanks to you and the boys' videos I've just started sponsoring a child through World Vision called

Priti :) Thank you for everything, hopefully I'll make my own video about it soon."

"This makes me wish I'd bothered to do something with my life instead of being another fat lazy douchebag watching YouTube videos."

World Vision is a brand that excels at telling compelling stories. But never before had a charity attempted to engage the YouTube audience in this way, partnering with vloggers to stir momentum around the cause of poverty alleviation. What made this a unique project was that we gave the vloggers—people not associated with World Vision—control over how the organization's work was depicted to a large audience. The Zambia trip allowed the vloggers to tell the story of World Vision's work, using their own words and lived experiences. This is the beauty of experiential marketing. There is nothing to hide. The vloggers and their viewers were allowed to experience and enjoy an intimate view of something truly amazing, something relevant to their interests and passions. World Vision could not have paid to create this type of brand advocacy.

The Vlogging Initiative Results

And here are some of the findings:

- The World Vision content that still lives has garnered 1.5 million views and assists with search engine marketing efforts.

- There have been 33,000 visits to the microsite hosting the videos (http://www.worldvisionvloggers.com) and requests for sponsorship.

- More than 11,000 comments on video content (this doesn't include comments shared via non-YouTube social networks) have been posted.

- Child sponsorships and donations provided a stronger return on investment than competing marketing channels. This was surprising, considering viewers were between 13 and 25 years old, and most donors begin sponsoring after they've found full-time employment.

- There is a potential for future donations from viewers currently too young to donate. With 1.5 million views on video content, the members of this young audience are primed to give when they are old enough to have disposable income.

The Vloggers' Perspective

We interviewed vloggers Shawna, Tom, and Alex, and here's what they had to say about the World Vision Zambia trip:

■ **Q. How did you feel when World Vision approached you to be a part of this project? Did it surprise you that this organization would want to involve vloggers?**

Alex. Yes, I thought it was very forward-thinking and that made me happy, because a lot of brands don't get it with YouTube. The genesis of the idea was that the ways that a lot of charities are promoted are very negative and ridden with guilt. To come up with something different was really cool.

Shawna. I was ecstatic to be considered. It was an amazing opportunity, one that not only went hand-in-hand with my brand (organic experience), but also let me publicly support a cause I could be passionate about. My audience was also excited to take the trip with me.

Tom. I was so excited to be approached. I already knew about World Vision and supported their work, so I was very happy to be able to help out.

■ **Q. Describe how you think this kind of experience differed from other kinds of product pitches that you've gotten from brands. Was it different?**

Tom. What World Vision proposed with the Zambia trip was entirely different from every other brand that had ever contacted me. It was the first time I ever partnered with a brand because the project was so cutting-edge.

Shawna. An organic experience is always preferable to a "product pitch." People don't watch YouTubers the same way they watch a commercial. They don't want to be sold to, they want to be interacted with, and it's very important for this interaction to be genuine. It's easy to tell when someone is given specific, stringent talking points, because it simply doesn't fit on the YouTube platform. It benefits neither the brand nor the viewer receiving the "pitch" if the control is taken away from the presenter. Creative freedom and genuine expression are a must in new media advertising.

Alex. With the World Vision vloggers trip, what we did in Zambia was a totally unique experience. I could never have just paid for that experience with any amount of money. And World Vision never said, "You have to make X amount of videos, or you have to do it on certain days"—we were free to do whatever we wanted. But because World Vision was so kind and supportive, we wanted to make videos about it.

■ **Q. How do you feel about presenting an experience like this to your subscribers? Was it difficult for you to make the decision to ally with this organization and present that to your audience?**

Alex. I knew I was going to be making videos about something that was really important and interesting to me. I wanted to share that with people, and if they didn't engage with it, then it didn't matter. Hopefully people engaged, and I know that was the case because I had people say (in comments and messages) that they started sponsoring a child after watching the videos.

Shawna. It's always difficult for me to align with a brand. As a content creator, I always worry my audience will feel I am being less genuine if I do something with a brand, even one that I personally support. I can only do my best to choose to work with brands that are personally applicable to me and to my brand, so that any question of a falsified experience is taken out of the picture.

■ **Q. How do you think your audience received the Zambia vlogs?**

Tom. My audience *loved* the Zambia vlogs! People were really interested and engaged. They enjoyed seeing what I was getting up to in Zambia, but they were also superinterested in what World Vision was doing there.

Alex. I think in general people found the Zambia trip really interesting because it is a completely different world, a completely different perspective.

Shawna. My audience enjoyed seeing the trip through my eyes and learning about the work being done there. Advertisers forget that people desperately want to experience another person's viewpoint. Real excitement and interest are contagious and very hard to simulate.

■ Q. Did this change anything about the way you think about vlogging and being an influencer online?

Shawna. It made me feel like I could talk about important issues without it coming across as preachy, which was a great lesson to learn. I think we all have a responsibility to stand up for things that are important to us and others, and the Zambia vlogs just solidified in my mind that my videos are a free space for what I want to share, whatever that might be.

Tom. I was very surprised at how much people got involved; I received comments and messages from people saying they had sponsored a child or donated money after seeing my videos. I never thought of myself as "influential," but I realized that I could definitely make a difference.

Alex. There were quite a lot of responses from people saying that they had sponsored a child after seeing the Zambia vlogs. That was really cool, and I knew I had made a difference. I also started sponsoring a child as a result of seeing World Vision's work.

■ Q. In your own words, how would you describe the overall experience of the Zambia trip?

Tom: The Zambia trip was so momentous, exciting, and interesting. It was really big! It certainly made me see World

Vision and my online presence in a very positive light. And I think it made my audience see me in a more positive light, too. The experience is something that will stay with me for my whole life.

Shawna. My experience with World Vision is the best brand alignment I've ever had. No other company has allowed me the freedom and understanding that World Vision did, and I would definitely hold it up as an example to other organizations on how to run a successful new media advertising campaign.

Alex. Going into it, I didn't really know what to expect. It was a lot more positive than I thought it would be. The people we met were really excited and friendly, even though they were dealing with far worse problems than anyone I had ever met. That was the most humbling thing to me. The Zambian people were some of the happiest people I had ever met.

Success with Vloggers

Working successfully with a vlogger requires two hugely important features:

1. **Creative control.** Let the vloggers have creative control over how they communicate your product to their audience. Vloggers are very good at what they do and are the most qualified people at finding innovative ways of working a product or brand into a YouTube video.

2. **Transparency.** Vloggers relate to viewers by emphasizing honesty and trust. This is why it is important to give vloggers the freedom to give their honest opinions about your brand or product. It is equally important that you let your vlogger state that, yes, your brand did approach them for the purpose of creating a vlog. Partnerships with no obligations and no strings attached are usually the only brand engagements that fly with vloggers.

And Action!

(1) Consider whether vloggers in your niche or industry could support your YouTube marketing efforts. (2) Evaluate whether your company could arrange experiential activities that would make compelling vlog content. (3) Conduct a search on both YouTube and Google to identify vloggers who operate in support of your niche or with the demographic of people that you want to reach. (4) Broker a deal with a vlogger to see if this style of marketing would work well for your brand. If so, scale up the program to drive significant engagement.

Mastering the Three On-Screen Formats

There are an incredible number of video styles that you can use to create good YouTube marketing content. But when you really boil it down, there are six basic forms that you'll most likely want to use. In this chapter, we'll walk through the first three that include on-screen work. Then in the next chapter, we'll walk through the three that don't include on-screen work.

Our goal here is to master each form in a simple yet professional manner. If you take a random stroll through YouTube, you'll notice how many videos fall into one of these six categories:

- **The anchorperson video.** Shot indoors with the presenter directly in front of the camera

- **The weatherperson video.** Shot outside in natural light with the presenter sharing on location

- **The hand model video.** Shot indoors with the camera pointed at the presenter's hands as he or she demonstrates something

- **The screen-capture video.** Captured on the computer with the presenter's voice being recorded as he or she explains what's happening on the computer screen

- **The movie trailer video.** Frequently associated with product launches; features still images of the product set to music

- **The product commercial video.** Focused on displaying the attributes of a product that you want to promote

Let's explore each on-screen style and break down the critical aspects. I'll use an example for each style from our business.

The Anchorperson Video

In this style of video, you stand in front of the camera like a TV anchorperson. In its simplest form, the anchorperson video can be shot using your computer's webcam or even your iPhone. Obviously, it can be shot with much more professional equipment to produce an effective style that looks as good as a TV studio's results. An anchorperson video is incredibly useful if you have a personal message that you want to share directly with your prospects. While some people prefer to shoot these videos sitting down, we've always preferred to shoot them standing up. Both styles are common on YouTube.

In our example (see Figure 8.1), Cinnamon created a video entry for the Bernina Brand Ambassador contest. In part of the video, she was on camera with a traditional weatherperson-style shot. In this example, the video was a mix of on-camera shots and movie trailer–style shots. When combined, the video was fast paced and entertaining. Did she win? Yep, and she also received a high-end sewing machine as well as the honor as serving as an official Brand Ambassador for the premiere German sewing machine company.

Elements of an Effective Anchorperson Video

The anchorperson video is fairly simple to put together. The camera doesn't need to move, nor are multiple camera angles required. It's just a straight-on camera shot.

Lighting
Because an anchorperson video is shot inside, you need to manage the lighting effectively to produce a good outcome. That won't happen by

Figure 8.1 Cinnamon using an anchorperson-style video

accident. The best possible indoor lighting arrangement is a mix of natural light and artificial light. The goal is to achieve a warm and bright appearance that's not harsh. In Seattle, where we live, it is occasionally hard to get a warm and bright lighting effect, especially in the winter months. Depending on the time of year, we lean more heavily on artificial light than you might need to. The easiest results are achieved when you can shoot directly in front of a large set of windows that allow for a lot of bright but indirect light.

Camera Arrangement

The easiest arrangement is to have the camera mounted on a tripod directly in front of you, with a distance to the camera of three to five feet depending on how much of a close-up shot you want. Generally, the entire torso is visible in an anchorperson video.

Background

The goal of the background is to create a professional mood and not distract. You'll notice that in our anchorperson video example in Figure 8.1, the background isn't ideal. We shot that video with Cinnamon standing in her office next to her whiteboard with some girl's drawing on it. Ideally, that would have been a cleaner background and therefore a more professional look. If we could have positioned her farther away from the wall, then more of the office would have been in view, which probably would have created a better look. In our case, shooting our videos in our home office, which isn't very big, is always a challenge.

Camera

Many cameras can shoot this type of video, with varying degrees of quality. The general rule is that if your lighting, camera arrangement, and background are effective, then your camera doesn't have to be particularly amazing. Obviously, the camera is one of the most important aspects of producing a professional-looking finished product. But don't allow yourself to fall into the mental trap of delaying your video work because you don't have the right camera. Let's review your camera options briefly:

- The simplest camera arrangement is to use the built-in camera on your computer. The quality won't be great, but depending on your audience expectations, this can be an acceptable option. As we've already mentioned, the lighting, camera arrangement, and background are critical, which is especially true if you are using your computer's built-in camera.

- A step up from the built-in camera would be a handheld camera. Your first option in this category is to use a small phone-based camera. While a few years ago this would have been unthinkable, the camera quality on phones continues to improve. There are phones that can shoot HD video that looks as good as or even better than the video shot by many camcorders on the market today. There is no reason you cannot shoot your videos with a newer iPhone. Our iPhone 5 produces very nice 1,080-pixel HD video.

> **POWER TIP**
>
> The term *1,080-pixel HD* is the abbreviated way of saying the video footage is shot using a high-definition video mode characterized by 1,080 horizontal lines of vertical resolution and progressive scanning instead of an older interlaced method. *Full HD* means the video quality includes a wide-screen aspect ratio of 16:9, creating a resolution of 1,920 by 1,080 pixels.

- A step up from a phone-based camera would be a handheld video camera. Today, the technology has progressed to the point of the traditional camcorder being all but obsolete. The newer DSLR (digital single-lens reflex) cameras shoot HD video with stunning quality. They have built-in sensors that enable incredible image quality and control of the depth of field. So if you feel compelled to have the highest production standards and truly stunning HD video, then consider purchasing a newer DSLR camera. The beauty of using a DSLR camera for your video work is that your lenses can be changed depending on the situation. We prefer the Canon line, but the Nikon line is also incredibly good.

Audio

The audio quality of your video is critical. Depending on the camera you use, you might be able to capture acceptable audio recordings. Generally, this is more likely for videos recorded inside. But to ensure you get good-quality audio, you might want to invest in an upgraded microphone solution. We have always used our video camera's microphone and have been reasonably happy with the outcome.

Introduction

Depending on the effect you're trying to achieve, you might want to create a video introduction. This can be done in a number of ways. During the editing process, you can simply insert a title clip. Or you can pay to have a more professional introduction done. On Fiverr.com, there are dozens of video production specialists who will create an animated video introduction for you. They provide you with the completed work as a video file, and in the editing process, you simply insert it before your recorded video clips. This produces a very nice and professional effect.

Editing

The nice part about an anchorperson video is that the editing is very easy. Because the performance is a monologue, with the presenter standing in the same place, editing is uncomplicated. Of course, you cannot easily fix problems with the lighting, background, or camera arrangement. So the editing process can't help you with those elements. But the editing process can help you trim down unwanted gaps in the video, awkward pauses, or unwanted comments.

The simplest way to quickly produce a good anchorperson video is to script it out in advance and film it in one sitting. If you do it in multiple sittings, then you run the risk of having the lighting, background, or other video elements look different from clip to clip. Having the presenter do the presentation in a few chunks rather than all in one take is also helpful. That way, if editing needs to occur to address problems, it is easier to accomplish. If the presenter does record the video in a few chunks, then editing will be required to make the final video look seamless. If you're working with a presenter who is very comfortable on camera and the video is relatively short, then it is possible to do the entire video in one take, which makes editing almost completely unnecessary.

The software you use to edit your video is a personal preference. For the last several years, we've used iMovie on our iMac. It is relatively easy to learn and can do everything we need. Before that, we used Windows Movie Maker. These are the simplest editing tools to use. Other popular options include Final Cut Pro and Sony Vegas Pro. Using editing software is like using any other computer software. The primary goal is to become proficient as quickly as possible. Once you know how to use the software without stress or frustration, you can focus on the creative process. Of course, the beautiful part about YouTube is that there are literally hundreds of tutorial videos about using each of these video editing software packages.

The Weatherperson Video

The weatherperson video (see Figure 8.2) is a style where you stand in front of the camera like a TV weatherperson. These videos are very similar to the anchorperson video except that they are shot outside on location.

Figure 8.2 Liberty on-screen in a weatherperson-style video. This was shot in our front yard.

Elements of an Effective Weatherperson Video

As with the anchorperson video, the weatherperson video is fairly simple to put together. The camera doesn't need to move, nor are multiple camera angles required. Just as for the anchorperson video, it's a straight-on camera shot. The biggest variable that must be factored into this type of shot is the weather. As you can imagine, in Seattle we don't get to do these videos all year. But a wintertime outdoor video can be a lot of fun, especially if it's snowing or there is snow on the ground.

Lighting

Because your weatherperson video is an outside project, you need to manage the natural light carefully. You want bright, indirect light. Too much shade, and the video will be dark. Too much direct light, and the video will look harsh. The goal is to achieve a warm and bright appearance, not harsh or washed out.

Shooting in midmorning or later in the afternoon will give you a better outcome than shooting at midday. In those cases, you want the presenter's face pointing in the direction of the light. You've probably heard of the photographer's reference to "the golden hour," the hour before the sun sets. This window of time usually produces very warm, indirect light, which makes outdoor photography lighting particularly beautiful. That lighting approach works for video as well.

Of course, you can supplement the natural light with artificial lighting that you set up on location. But for most YouTube-level video work, I'm going to suggest that you don't need to do this unless you are in particularly difficult lighting situations.

Camera Arrangement

As with the anchorperson video, the camera arrangement is very straightforward. The presenter can be directly in front of the camera or slightly off to the side. A tripod can be used, although if done carefully, someone can simply hold the camera.

Background

The background for the weatherperson video is where you can add a lot of excitement and drama. We have the privilege of living in a lake community, so shooting videos down by the dock or next to the water is easy. That type of background adds a level of energy and interest to videos that is very effective. Of course, the background shouldn't distract from the presentation; it should complement it.

Camera

Generally, your indoor camera solution is the same one you'll use when shooting outdoors. That has always worked for us. Frequently, there are settings you'll want to choose on your camera to distinguish between the two locations. Your camera can do the adjustments for you if you learn the automatic settings. Recently, we've begun using our iPhone 5 in some outdoor situations, and the results have been good.

Audio

Whereas the lighting is the biggest challenge with indoor video work, the audio is frequently the biggest challenge with outdoor video work. Frequently, you'll be unable to control the background noise when you're shooting outside. So you'll have to manage that closely. It's not uncommon to shoot video on location, then in the editing process discover that the neighbor's lawnmower or an airplane or birds chirping are a significant distraction. As with most aspects of video production, practice makes perfect.

In most situations, you'll want to manage the location carefully to ensure a very quiet background. But this is not always the case. Sometimes you want the sounds of the location to be included to add interest to the video. If you're shooting your video at the football game or Times Square or the zoo, then the background noises can be a fun part of the final video.

Editing

The editing issues for a weatherperson video are the same as for the anchorperson video. The goal is to trim down unwanted gaps in the video, awkward pauses, or unwanted comments.

The Hand Model Video

The hand model video (see Figure 8.3) is a style that features your hands demonstrating something. This is a very common style for tutorials or how-to videos. You'll see it commonly used in the music lesson, gardening, crafting, cooking, and hair and beauty niches. The nice part about this video style is that it gives the watcher a bird's-eye view of the activity. This "over-the-shoulder" style of video is great for teaching people new things.

Elements of a Hand Model Video

The hand model video is usually done indoors, so it has similar requirements to those of the anchorperson video. If it's being shot outdoors, as an over-the-shoulder gardening tutorial for example, then it has the same requirements as a weatherperson video. Generally, the camera doesn't need to move, nor are multiple camera angles required. It's simply a straight-on camera shot.

Figure 8.3 Cinnamon using a hand model-style video

Lighting

The lighting requirements are generally the same as those for the anchorperson video when shot indoors. Special care needs to be taken with the brightness of the light to ensure that the activity being demonstrated can be clearly seen.

Camera Arrangement

As with the anchorperson video, the easiest arrangement is to mount the camera on a tripod. But in this case, the tripod would generally be over your shoulder, pointing down at your work surface. This can take some trial and error to get right, and sometimes it can put you in an awkward seating arrangement. But when done properly, it produces a tight close-up where the hands are prominent on the screen.

Background

The background for the hand model video is straightforward. The work surface becomes the background. Depending on the effect you are hoping to achieve, you can spend some time considering how to make the work surface look clean, professional, and interesting. In this type of video, your work surface implies something about the professionalism of your office and business. So make it look impressive.

Camera

Generally, the hand model video requires nothing different than an anchorperson video does. The only exception might be in cases where you are working on something in very close proximity and want a specialty lens that can produce a very tight shot. In this case, a DSLR camera with a macro lens is the preferred arrangement.

Audio

Managing the audio quality of your hand model video can be surprisingly tricky for several reasons. First, your camera (and therefore the camera mic) is probably over your shoulder. So it may have a hard time picking up good audio. Second, if you are using equipment such as a sewing machine or power tool, then the noise might be problematic. When we do hand model videos related to sewing, Cinnamon will frequently present, then demonstrate using the machine with no talking, then stop the machine and present more. In this way, the machine's noise isn't competing with the speaking parts. You'll have to do a little planning to decide how to solve the audio issues related to your own hand model videos.

Editing

The editing work for a hand model video can be different from that of the other video styles. The reason is simple. Usually in this type of video, you are trying to teach people something. So the step-by-step nature of the teaching is critical. You want to edit so the steps are clear and easily understood and flow together nicely.

On top of this step-by-step editing requirement, you still need to edit to remove the gaps, pauses, and awkward sections. The overall effect should be a seamless video that is both logical in its teaching outcome and seamless in its editing.

And Action!

(1) Evaluate your video needs and begin working on your preferred video style. (2) Consider what will best serve your audience and also what you can comfortably accomplish. (3) If you hate the idea of being on-screen, then consider the hand model–style video, or stick around till the next chapter when we'll discuss more options for being off-screen. (4) Purchase your camera, lighting, and editing software. (5) Shoot a practice video and begin learning how to manage the elements that go into making it great, including lighting, camera arrangement, audio, background, and editing.

Chapter 9

Mastering the Three
Off-Camera Video Formats

I n this chapter, we're going to continue to walk through video styles and focus on the videos where you aren't on camera. The off-camera form can be very enjoyable and stress-free, since it allows you to produce videos without feeling compelled to drop 20 pounds before you step in front of the camera.

Rather than obsessing over your own appearance, you can focus on how to make a high-quality video that will serve your prospects and customers effectively. While these video styles won't work for every niche or industry, they are very flexible, and with some creativity, you can most likely figure out how to apply them in your context. Let's review the three styles.

The Screen-Capture Video

The screen-capture video is a style that doesn't actually take a video camera to produce. It's a recording of your computer screen combined with your narration of what you're doing. Viewers are watching your computer screen as if they're looking over your shoulder. Screen-capture videos are particularly popular for the following fields:

the gaming industry, where these videos are frequently used to do game walk-throughs; the software industry, where they are used to do tutorials; and the educational industry, where they are used to do presentations about educational topics.

Elements of an Effective Screen-Capture Video

Screen-capture videos are easy to create once you have the right software. You simply prepare to show your computer screen and record your voice. If done well, you can end up with a very educational and personable video.

Software

Screen-capture videos are made possible by software that records your computer monitor. We have used and recommend Camtasia Studio by TechSmith. You can purchase the software for either a PC or Mac, and it is easy to learn. There are tutorials on YouTube if you need a lesson on how to use it. You can try the software for free as a trial or purchase a copy for $99.

POWER TIP

Rather than doing random or one-off screen-capture presentations, consider being very consistent with your format and style. Many YouTube channel owners have created massive followings by using the same look and feel in their screen-capture formats and simply exploring the next logical topic. This "liturgy" allows watchers to have confidence in what they're going to get when they subscribe. They become familiar with what to expect. It also allows you to focus on the topics, rather than stressing over the delivery. If there is no unique creative approach required to make your next video, you can make your videos faster. Find a format that people like, and simply rinse and repeat.

Screen-Capture Presentation

The primary question to resolve when you're going to create a screen-capture video is what are you going to display on the screen while you speak. There are lots of choices, including:

- A specific piece of software as you demonstrate it

- Your website as you discuss it

- Presentation software, such as PowerPoint, as you give a speech or demonstration

- Art or design software as you draw things and explain them

The options are only limited by your imagination. And if you are particularly unhappy with your on-screen presentation, you can always hire a freelancer to create an inspiring presentation or drawing based on your recorded audio track.

Audio

The audio recording quality associated with a screen-capture video is particularly important. To ensure a high-quality recording, you can upgrade from using your computer's built-in microphone to using a microphone that plugs into your computer's USB drive. A popular microphone for this purpose is the Blue Yeti microphone. It's the one we personally use, and it works very well.

Editing

The screen-capture video (see Figure 9.1) still requires editing like a traditional video, but instead of editing video footage, you're editing screen-captured footage. The goal remains the same: to ensure that pauses, gaps, and awkwardly worded sections are cleaned up.

The Movie Trailer Video

If you have an exciting event coming up, then a movie trailer–style video might be a useful tool. In a movie trailer video, your goal is to reveal something exciting and new. It might be a product, a new service, or a new website or physical location.

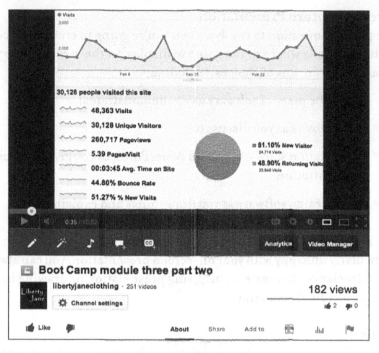

Figure 9.1 Jason using a screen-capture video style as part of a social media boot camp

Elements of an Effective Movie Trailer Video

The movie trailer video (see Figure 9.2) is effective when it announces something new in a way that is exciting and fun for the intended audience. A video designed for mid-career CPAs is going to look very different from one created for 13-year-old girls. So this type of video is highly dependent on your audience. But overall, the goal is to do a big reveal in a fun and exciting manner.

Movie trailer videos can be a combination of video styles and can include an on-screen presentation, like the anchorperson video. Other styles to consider integrating include demonstration-style videos, such as the hand model video, or animation and screen-capture elements with voice-over, as with screen-capture videos. These styles can be mixed together to create an effective presentation that reveals your exciting new thing.

Editing

Editing a movie trailer–style video is a bit more complicated than other styles since the degree of professionalism will depend on the editing choices. If there is one video style you might consider outsourcing, it's this one.

Figure 9.2 Using a movie trailer–style video for our product launch

If you want to create a brief movie trailer video yourself, then consider using the movie trailer function in iMovie. It produces fairly good results by simply combining the footage and still pictures you have available.

The Commercial Video

The commercial video is a brief commercial for your new product or service. Rather than simply revealing the product or service as would be done in a movie trailer video, the commercial video focuses on presenting benefits and features. It sells the new product or service in a brief and compelling way.

Elements of an Effective Commercial Video

The commercial video is designed to do one thing—show the benefits and features of your new product or service. It's a selling tool. It might contain still images as well as product footage—or even on-screen presentations, à la the anchorperson video.

Music

The commercial-style video is one that will frequently require music to make the video feel professional and polished. This presents another element that is important to master: the use of professionally recorded music. As you're probably aware, using music when you don't hold the copyright is problematic for businesses. Whereas you can include music in your personal videos without much concern about being sued, in a business context, this is a serious concern.

The best way to ensure you have good music to include in your video is to use music with a Creative Commons license. And even within the Creative Commons process, you need to ensure that the specific piece of music you want to use allows business uses. To find a wide assortment of music currently published under Creative Commons licenses, visit these sites:

- ccMixter.org
- FreeMusicArchive.org
- Jamendo.com

Editing

Editing commercial videos is similar to editing the movie trailer videos. The professionalism, appeal, and overall quality of the video will largely come down to the editing. As with the movie trailer video, this is one that you might want to hand over to a professional videographer and editor.

Close Up with My Froggy Stuff

The members of the team at My Froggy Stuff have created an amazing YouTube following by focusing on craft projects for dolls (see Figure 9.3). They shoot all their videos using the hand model style that we talked about in Chapter 8. At the time of this writing, they have 172,000 subscribers and 105 million video views. You can see their current statistics at http://www.youtube.com/user/MyFroggyStuff. We asked "Froggy" and "Froggy Mama" (respectively, daughter and mother in real life) to help us understand how they approach YouTube.

Figure 9.3 The My Froggy Stuff YouTube channel About page

▦ Q. Your tutorials are incredible—how did all this start?

A. I grew up in a crafty home. My mom and I were always making or repainting something, from furniture to Christmas ornaments, and when I had a little girl of my own, the tradition just kind of continued. My husband was in the military, causing us to move frequently and keeping us far away from family, so my daughter and I started making stuff together for her dolls, and we would make videos to show our family how we did it. After a while, we noticed that other people found our videos useful, and it all just kind of snowballed from there.

▦ Q. When did you first envision having a YouTube channel for your work?

A. We opened our first YouTube channel for personal use, you know, for watching videos and sharing our latest creations with the family. After a while, we noticed we had a growing audience, so we switched gears, removed all the personal stuff, and focused on crafts and "The Darbie Show." I never really considered myself to be an artist or considered what I did to be work; we were just having fun, and YouTube was a great avenue to share our creations.

Q. Do you consider your YouTube efforts to be a business?

A. At first no, it was just pure creative fun. We did our best to push our creative limits and have a blast at the same time. However, the growth kind of pushed us into a business frame of mind, but we make sure to keep "fun" at the heart of everything we do.

Q. What specific steps have you taken to boost your YouTube results?

A. The instant feedback we get from our audience is like gold. We make sure we take the time to read the comments so that we know what they liked, what they didn't, and what they would like to see. The comments really help to keep us current and relevant to our audience, and we try to accommodate when we can without compromising our own values. Plus, we think it is important to stay connected with our audience, to let them know that we are listening and that we care about what they have to say.

Q. What were some of your early challenges or struggles?

A. Keeping up with the comments and time management. After a while, the sheer volume was a tad overwhelming, and some of the negative comments had a little bite. I (Froggy) also had to find a balance between giving the audience what they wanted and my creative freedom.

Q. How did you overcome them?

A. I had to realize that it was impossible to please everyone and that I needed help to manage the comments. That is when I went to my mom, the woman who sparked my creative juices (Froggy Mama), and asked her for help. And boy, did she! She became the "mama" of the site, policing the comments and creating "The Request List" so that I could glance at the topics to get ideas of where to go with the next video. This all really helped to streamline the process and keep me focused. Down the road, we required more help, so we developed a little Froggy Team of myself (Froggy), Little Froggy (my daughter), Froggy Boy, Froggy Mama, Papa Frog, and Chris B.

▪ Q. What "aha" moments have you experienced where you realized you could do something differently/better to boost your YouTube results?

A. After we created the Froggy Team and delegated responsibilities, I found myself with a ton of free time, which meant, of course—more videos! And more videos made our audience happy, which in turn made our audience grow.

▪ Q. What business or personal results or successes have you achieved because of YouTube?

A. I am able to create something wonderful with the people I love and trust. My daughter, mom, and I have this tremendous bond where we laugh and giggle over scripts and craft projects. My son is delighted to scream "Happy Crafting!" at the end of our videos, and even my dad and husband (two of our greatest supporters) now know more about dolls than they probably ever thought they would. Our family has really connected over all of this, and to me, this is our success.

▪ Q. Is advertising revenue your primary business goal?

A. We have a more of a social goal rather than a business goal. We hope to spark creativity and positivity through our videos and all that we do. However, I will not deny that business success is icing on the cake.

■ **Q. If you were sitting down with someone just getting started on YouTube, what advice would you give?**

A. What I always suggest to people who ask me that question is to do something they love, create the videos they enjoy, and the right people will find them. If you are passionate about your work, then you are more likely to stick with it through all the obstacles and challenges, and the work will be fulfilling whether you have one subscriber or a million. YouTube allows us to be original, creative, and expressive, so I say let your message be your driving force.

■ **Q. What common mistakes do you see people making on YouTube?**

A. I think that the concern to gain subscribers can distract some from making original content, and without the good content, it is hard to retain those subscribers.

■ **Q. What are the biggest mistakes you've made using YouTube that we can help folks avoid?**

A. For me, it was letting the negative comments get to me. There would be tons of positive statements, but I would single out the one negative or hurtful comment and dwell on it, wasting valuable time wondering what I did wrong. What I *was* doing wrong was giving time and attention to something that had no value. Nonconstructive criticism is a waste of time designed to distract you, so just hit the delete button and keep going. Focus on the positive and not the negative.

■ **Q. Can you distill your YouTube advice down into several key tips for readers?**

A. ■ Be original.

■ Consistently produce content.

■ Interact with your audience.

- Stay focused and remember why you started, but don't be afraid to try new things.

- Keep it fun.

Putting It All Together

In the last three chapters, we've explored how to get video bloggers to help you create content for your business. We've also explored six video styles that are commonly used. Take the time to identify the top two video formats that you believe will work for your business. Get laser-beam-focused on how to accomplish making videos using those formats. Look for examples from other companies that use those two video formats. Don't be distracted or overwhelmed by all the possibilities—simply focus on developing a content pipeline that brings those videos to your audience as quickly and efficiently as possible. Own those styles and work to become a master producer.

And Action!

(1) Determine an off-camera video style that will work in support of your brand, products, or industry. (2) If screen-capture videos are a good option for your work, then pick up a copy of Camtasia from TechSmith. (3) Identify a style that your fans or prospects enjoy and use it faithfully. Your "liturgy" will be comforting to subscribers and make video production simpler. (4) Learn from Froggy and Froggy Mama and focus on making original content, consistently producing new content, interacting with your audience, and staying focused while keeping it fun.

THE
SUCCESSFUL
SETUP

YouTube

YouTube Channel Setup and Best Practices

Your YouTube channel is an expression of your brand, just like your website or Facebook fan page. You get to decide how the graphic art, videos, and video titles all work together to establish your brand on YouTube. Your goal is to create a version of your brand on the platform that people will click with immediately and recognize as authentically you.

Fortunately, the YouTube team gives you a nice set of options to arrange things effectively. It is important to note that YouTube updated its channel format substantially in the spring of 2013, so if you're not familiar with the new standards and layout options, this chapter will get you up to speed.

The One Channel Design Refresh

One of the primary goals of the spring 2013 update was to ensure that YouTube viewers and content publishers had a good experience on the various screen sizes, including TV, desktops, tablets, and smartphones. YouTube called this new channel refresh the "One Channel" design. With the new channel format, YouTube has done all the hard work for us to ensure our brands are presented nicely on each of these types of screens. But in order to maximize the value of the new design, we've got to do a few things, too. In this chapter, we'll walk through the basic account setup procedures and best practices for the new channel format. If you already have a YouTube channel, then you can skip the setup procedures and jump to the "Configuring Your New YouTube Channel Effectively" section.

Setting Up Your Google and YouTube Accounts

In order to sign up for a YouTube account, you must have a Google account.

Setting Up Your Google Account

Signing up for a Google account is easy at https://accounts.google.com /SignUp. When you sign up for a Google account, you are given a Gmail e-mail address. With it, you get access to a whole set of programs, including:

- Gmail
- Google Groups
- Picasa
- Chrome
- Google+
- Blogger
- Hangouts
- YouTube

Setting Up Your YouTube Account

Now that you've got a Google account, you can sign in to YouTube using your new Gmail address. One of the first things you'll want to do is set up a custom channel name and then set up your channel's artwork. If you don't, your channel won't look branded in any way (see Figure 10.1).

Let's walk through how to create a custom channel name; then we'll discuss how to add customizable elements to your new YouTube channel.

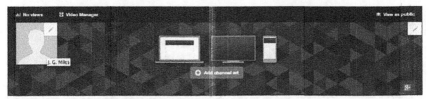

Figure 10.1 Your channel won't look very personalized until you add artwork.

Getting Your Custom URL

You rarely get assigned a channel name that is useful—the URL assigned will be a random set of numbers. But this is easily solved. You just have to go to the additional step of setting up a unique channel name, also known as a "custom" or "vanity" URL. It will change your YouTube channel URL from something like http://www.youtube.com/channel/UCo PBhcZ70buZTaNPF5K8xMg to something like http://www.youtube .com/libertyjanemedia.

Steps for Setting Up a Custom URL

To set up your custom URL, you go to your YouTube settings (as seen in Figure 10.2), which are found under your account name in the top right corner of your YouTube page.

Jason G. Miles	0	
YouTube	**Google account**	
My channel	Profile	Jason G. Miles
Video Manager	Google+	
Subscriptions	Privacy	Sign out
YouTube settings	Settings	Switch account

Figure 10.2 Selecting the YouTube settings will allow you to access your account information.

In the YouTube settings area, you'll see your account information, as in Figure 10.3. Just below your name, you'll notice a link to "Change to a business or other name, and disconnect Google+ profile." Simply click that link to open the Change to a Business dialogue box.

Figure 10.3 In the Account Information area, you can select the option to change to a business channel.

In the dialogue box, you have the option of exploring potential names and seeing if they are currently available on YouTube (see Figure 10.4). This may take some creative thinking and a clear vision of your branding concept. You don't want to act hastily in this step, as you can only do it one time—so you've got to get it right the first time. Once the name is chosen, it will replace your personal name on your YouTube channel. In my case, the new URL will be https://www.youtube.com /libertyjanemedia. And on my YouTube channel, my name will be displayed as it was created, libertyjanemedia.

Change to a business or other name, and disconnect Google+ profile

Choose a name for your channel
Username: Check availability

| |

Your username can contain only letters and numbers.

On YouTube

• The name you enter will replace Jason G. Miles on your channel.
• The name you enter here will also become your channel URL. **This cannot be changed later.**

On Google+

• Your profile will still exist, with your name on it (**Jason G. Miles**), but you can delete or modify it later.
• Your Google+ profile will be disconnected from your YouTube channel.

Cancel   OK

Figure 10.4 The Choose a Name dialogue box

The final step in completing your custom URL setup is to go to your YouTube channel and ensure the new name is properly formatted for visitors to see. YouTube places your new custom URL name on your YouTube channel as the channel name, but they are separate items. Your URL can be different from your channel name. If your URL is one word and that is what you want your channel to be named, then you'll have nothing to fix. But if it's more than one word or if you want another name, then you'll need to edit the name. Spaces are not automatically added when it is set up, so be sure to add them if you need them. You'll also want to capitalize the letters properly. In my example, the new custom channel name appeared as libertyjanemedia, and I wanted it to be Liberty Jane Media. To make changes like this, you simply click on the pencil icon next to your name and edit the wording.

Configuring Your New YouTube Channel Effectively

Now that you've set up your account and selected your custom URL, it's time to start adding the elements that will help your channel be well branded.

Setting Up the Channel Icon

The channel icon is located in the upper left corner of the YouTube header. Until you add an image, it will have a light-blue silhouette. Generally for businesses, this would be the perfect spot to install your logo. You add it by clicking on the pencil icon as you hover your mouse over the image. You'll have the option of uploading an image that is no greater than 1 megabyte, and dimensions should be 800 pixels square. Or you can simply take a video still from one of your uploaded videos. It is probably wisest to upload a copy of your logo, or if you're an entrepreneur, maybe you should upload a headshot.

Creating the Channel Art

The channel art is your primary banner image across the top of your channel page. You update it by clicking on the pencil icon in the top right corner of the header area. You can upload your own image or use a stock photo that YouTube provides. If you upload your own image, then you need to ensure that the size of the image is 2,560 pixels by 1,440 pixels. The maximum file size is 2 megabytes. Your channel art can be a creative combination of text and imagery to make a unique and well-branded presentation of your company. In my example (see Figure 10.5), I made up a quote and used a public domain picture. I put them together in Photoshop Elements, saved the result as a PNG file, and then uploaded it. You might want to use a product shot or image of your offices or stores—whatever helps position you properly with your target audience.

Figure 10.5 When you update your artwork and links, your page starts to look pretty good.

> **POWER TIP**
>
> Not sure how to make a good channel art image that will look professional and trendy? Don't want to learn how to use Photoshop Elements? Go to Fiverr.com and simply pay someone to do it for you for $5. Look under the "Graphics & Design" section and ensure you are getting a layout for the new One Channel design format. There are designers waiting to help you. Problem solved.

The other item you can update when you click on the pencil icon in the top right corner is the channel links. You'll want to update your social links, as well as include a link to your website.

Updating Your Social Links

The social links refer to icons for your various social media sites. You can add links for many sites, including:

- Google+
- Facebook
- Twitter
- Myspace
- Tumblr
- Instagram
- Pinterest
- Flickr

You'll notice that on my fully set-up channel, I've included social links to my profiles on Instagram, Facebook, Pinterest, and Sound-Cloud.

Adding a Link to Your Website

You also get the option to create a clickable link to your website, or if you'd like, you can link to another YouTube channel. You can create a name and associate a URL with it. Generally you'd link to your website, but the alternative is also an interesting option. Linking to another channel would make sense if you have multiple channels and you want to cross-promote from one to the other. If you're focused on driving traffic from YouTube to your website, then you'll want to use your company's website.

Instead of just pointing this website link to your top-level domain name, consider where you might want new YouTube visitors to enter your website and point the link to that destination, or "deep link" within your site. In our case, instead of linking to http://www.pixiefaire .com, our doll clothes patterns site, we might link to http://www.pixie faire.com/collections/free-doll-clothes-patterns, our site for free doll clothes patterns.

Setting Up the Channel Trailer Video

The channel trailer is a relatively new YouTube feature that allows you to have a promotional video that is displayed to visitors who are not currently subscribers to your channel, and it's an opportunity for you to customize a video that will appeal directly to these people.

To set up the channel trailer, simply click on the pencil icon next to your channel name and choose the Edit Channel Navigation option. The first option is to enable the default view. This will give you the ability to add a trailer video to your channel. Once you have the option to add a channel trailer video, simply choose the video you'd like to feature. It will appear just below the four tabs Home, Videos, Discussion, and About.

The Four Navigation Tabs

Just below your name on your YouTube channel, you'll notice the four tabs. These are the primary navigation paths that your visitors will take when engaging with your channel. Let's briefly look at each:

- **The Home tab.** Allows visitors to navigate back to your primary channel page.

- **The Videos tab.** Lists all the videos you've uploaded. It is also the tab where you can create a playlist, which is a useful feature we'll discuss later in this chapter.

- **The Discussion tab.** Is one of the primary social attributes of YouTube. You can receive and reply to comments left on your channel.

- **The About tab.** Provides a place to add a description of your channel and a link to your website.

Writing a Channel Description

The channel description is located on the About tab. This is your opportunity to explain who you are and what your business is all about. You only have 1,000 words, so be sure to use effective copywriting to tell your story in that limited amount of space. You also want to write for maximum "discoverability," meaning to write in a way that places your important keywords toward the front of the description.

Displaying Statistics

You have the option to display your channel statistics or not. The two statistics that are available to be displayed are the number of subscribers and the number of video views. If you choose to display them, these statistics will show up on your About tab.

Featuring Other Channels

Another feature you can customize is the display of other YouTube channels that you want to feature. These are also displayed on the About tab and are generally used to cross-promote channels that you work with.

Focusing on Discoverability

The channel title, URL, and description are all key aspects of search engine optimization (SEO) work. And since Google owns YouTube, you'll want to pay special attention to the issues related to SEO. You always want to write with your visitors in mind, but also consider how best to include important keywords. If done well, your new visitors will understand what you are all about, and Google's search algorithm will, too.

Exploring the Banner Header

The banner header is the section at the top of your channel art. It is visible to you as the channel owner, but it is not to your viewers or subscribers. On the banner header, you'll find the following information:

- **Subscribers.** The number of channel subscribers

- **Views.** The total number of video views your channel has received since its creation

- **Video Manager.** A link to your video managing tool, which you use to upload and edit your videos as well as manage your playlists

- **View as Public.** A button that allows you to view your channel as the public views it

Working with Playlists

Playlists are a collection of videos that you think your subscribers will enjoy viewing. Creating a playlist is a way to elegantly organize your content by topic, theme, product line, or any other relevant method. Your playlists can serve as navigational shortcuts for your customers.

To set up a playlist, simply click on the Playlists button in the left-hand navigation column on your channel. Then click Create a Playlist and then +New Playlist. You have the option of giving the playlist a name and providing a description.

Connecting Social Accounts

As mentioned at the beginning of this chapter, YouTube allows you to connect your Facebook and Twitter accounts to your new channel. You can then allow your YouTube activities to be automatically published on those sites. You can create automatic updates for the following activities:

- Uploading videos

- Adding videos to public playlists

- Commenting on videos

- Liking videos

Obviously, these options give you an opportunity to create and manage content across several of your social media platforms in an interesting way. In Part 4, we'll discuss this further as we talk about best practices for integrating YouTube into your entire social media mix.

Your Feed Is Born

YouTube refers to the stream of your activity as your "feed." It is broadcast to your subscribers. The default settings for your feed include sharing:

- Uploads

- Liked videos

- Videos added to playlists

- Bulletins

- Comments you make

- Channels to which you subscribe

- "Favorited" videos

Your feed is designed to keep your subscribers updated but not overwhelmed with news of your activities. But you'll want to monitor this and adjust settings as needed to ensure you don't overload your subscribers. YouTube does some of this work for you, for example, by bundling activities such as uploading a video and then commenting on it.

The broadcast features also help you solve the opposite problem. If you are not publishing new videos frequently but you want to remain active and engaged with your YouTube subscribers, then your feed will help. You can comment on videos, add them to a playlist, or add someone else's video to a post on your channel. This strategy is particularly empowering if you are serving as a coach or educator on YouTube, as we described in Chapter 5.

Putting It All Together

If you've walked through the steps outlined in this chapter to get your channel set up and organized, and if you've done the positioning and video strategy work outlined in Chapters 4 through 9, then you're ready to have a vibrant and engaging YouTube marketing program. If we put it all together, then you should have these items fully completed:

- Your shiny new YouTube channel set up and ready to use (this chapter)

- A clear understanding of the size and scope of YouTube and how it works (Chapter 1)

- Clarity on the value of a YouTube marketing strategy and how your business will benefit by doing this marketing work (Chapter 2)

- An understanding of the challenges and struggles that businesses face when trying to establish a YouTube marketing strategy (Chapter 3)

- A solid understanding of the type of content you should be publishing—content that will resonate with the people in your target audience and serve their self-interest (Chapter 4)

- Knowledge of how to position your brand and create the persona you desire (Chapter 5)

- A game plan for how to get your pipeline of videos up and running (Chapters 6 and 7)

- A clear understanding of how to master the on-camera as well as off-camera video styles that are commonly used on YouTube (Chapters 8 and 9)

In the second half of this book, we will focus all our energy on the best practices for driving traffic from YouTube onto our websites and related sales pages. Let's be honest; we aren't creating a YouTube marketing strategy for kicks. We're doing it so we can systematically drive lots of qualified prospects toward purchasing decisions. We're doing it to grow our businesses' revenues. And the great news is that there are lots of ways to do it. Let's dig into those in the upcoming chapters.

And Action!

(1) Set up your YouTube channel if you don't have one yet. (2) Claim your custom URL. (3) Create your channel icon and channel art so that your brand is well positioned on your new channel. (4) Set up your channel's information in a way that makes your work easily discoverable. (5) Begin managing your feed effectively, so you can curate and create content that will attract subscribers.

Uploading Videos to YouTube

N ow that you've got your channel created and your video pipe-line figured out, it's time to get familiar with the uploading and video management aspects of YouTube. In this chapter, we'll walk through how to upload videos as well as explore the features and functions associated with managing a video.

Upload Your First Video to YouTube

Uploading your first video to YouTube is easy. Understanding what choices are involved and how to best use the various features takes a bit more time to learn. As with all new things, your comfort level at the beginning will be low and your stress will be high. But over time, those two emotions reverse, and you'll be uploading videos quickly and in a stress-free way. If you'd like to see YouTube's official resource section for video creators, visit http://www.youtube.com/yt/creators/. Let's look at the basic steps, and then we'll talk about useful options and features.

1. Visit your YouTube channel and make sure you're logged in. You know you're logged in when you see your user name in the top right corner.

2. To the left of your name, you'll see the Upload button with a drop-down icon. Click Upload to go directly to the Upload tool. If you click the drop-down menu, you'll be given different options that are somewhat unrelated to uploading your new video. YouTube has created many options for uploading videos (see Figure 11.1).

- **Webcam Capture option.** This option allows you to record directly from your webcam to quickly create an anchorperson-style video.

- **Photo Slideshow option.** This tool allows you to build a slide show and quickly upload it.

- **Google+ Hangouts on Air option.** Capturing a Google+ Hangout and saving it as a video is simple with this integration tool. You just set up the broadcast and hit the Record button, and you're off to the races. This is ideal for an interview-style video.

- **Upload a Public Video setting.** This is the most common setting used by video creators. It allows you to pick a video you've previously saved and list it on your channel publicly. When you upload a public video, your subscribers are notified in their feeds.

- **Upload an Unlisted Video setting.** This feature is incredibly helpful if you want to make a video for a selected audience and now have that video publicly available. The unlisted video won't show up in YouTube's public spaces. It won't be displayed on your channel, in search results, or on the YouTube home page. The video is only available to people who have the video's URL. So simply upload the unlisted video; then e-mail your target audience a link to it.

- **Upload a Private Video setting.** A private video is even more secure than an unlisted video. When you upload a private video, you are given access to a field under the privacy settings where you can add up to 50 people who can view the video. This is done via their YouTube user names or e-mail addresses, but they'll need to have a YouTube user name to view the video. This option is great for team projects and private uses of YouTube for business collaboration.

- **Schedule a Video option.** If you want to be very faithful in uploading your videos at regular intervals, then using this feature could be very helpful. The scheduled video will show up in people's feeds and on your playlists based on the scheduled time, not the actual uploaded time.

3. Once you've selected the type of video you want to upload, you can simply click the "Select files to upload" icon. You'll be provided with a file browser. When you choose the file you want to upload, it will automatically begin. You can confirm that the setting you wanted (public, private, or unlisted) is correctly chosen. You'll also see the graph showing the progress of the upload. It may take a few minutes.

4. The screen you're looking at during the upload process also allows you to edit the basic information of the video. You'll notice that there are two other tabs, Monetization and Advanced Settings. Let's look at the basic video information, then the secondary tabs:

- **Video title.** This is likely the most important metadata associated with your video. Although no one outside of YouTube knows the exact algorithm used for creating search engine results, the title is the most obvious aspect of meaningful search results. Remember, YouTube is the second largest search engine only behind Google. So name your video wisely.

- **Description.** The description of your video allows people to see exactly what it is about. This space also allows you to include a clickable URL. So if your video is associated with a product or similar selling effort, then include a link to the relevant e-commerce page. Note that the description field will truncate your content. So put the URL and the most vital information in the first sentence or two.

- **Tags.** The tags in YouTube allow you to declare the relevant topics that people will find in your video. These are separated by commas and should include all the relevant subject matter from your video. Use YouTube's Keyword Suggestion tool to identify relevant tags. You can find it at https://www.youtube.com/keyword_tool.

- **Video Thumbnails option.** During the upload process, YouTube will take three screenshots of your video. You can select the one you'd like to have as your thumbnail image. Or you can upload your own custom image, with a maximum size of two megabytes.

- **Privacy Settings tab.** You'll also notice that you are given a drop-down box that allows you to change the privacy settings of your video. If you uploaded it as unlisted, but now you want to make it public, you can do that here.

- **Monetization tab options.** The Monetization tab allows you to choose to monetize your video. Once you accept the terms, you will be given a menu of monetization options. We'll discuss these options in greater detail in an upcoming chapter.

- **Syndication options.** The second part of the monetization options is related to where your video will be displayed. The syndication options include "everywhere" or "monetized platforms." If you choose "everywhere," your video will be displayed on all available platforms. If you choose "monetized platforms," it will only appear on those platforms that allow your videos to be monetized.

- **Advanced Setting tabs.** The advanced settings allow you to control a lot of the user-related options for your video, including:

  - **Comments & Responses check boxes.** Choices in this section include allowing comments, allowing users to vote on comments, allowing users to view ratings for the video, and allowing video responses.

  - **Caption Certification box.** This drop-down menu provides choices related to whether your video has been previously published. According to YouTube, "Content that has aired on U.S. television may be subject to FCC regulations regarding closed captions."

  - **Distribution option for embedding.** This menu option allows you to choose whether website owners can take your video and embed it on their sites.

- **Distribution option for notification of subscribers.** This option allows your subscribers to be notified. They will see your videos on their homepages and in their e-mails. This option is selected as yes by default.

- **Category options.** The category options allow you to choose the YouTube category that is most appropriate for your video. Choices include "Autos & Vehicles," "Comedy," "Education," "Entertainment, Film & Animation," "Gaming," "Howto & Style," "Music," "News & Politics," "Nonprofits & Activism," "People & Blogs," "Pets & Animals, "Science & Technology," "Sports," and "Travel & Events."

- **Video Location box.** The video location feature allows you to identify the physical location your video was shot at, such as Seattle, New York, Boston, etc.

- **Recording Date box.** The recording date option allows you to indicate when your video was recorded, as opposed to when it was uploaded to YouTube.

- **3D Video box.** The 3D Video option allows you to disable 3D for your video. Additionally, you can request YouTube make your video 3D or inform YouTube that your video is already 3D. Or you can simply ignore this option and not state a preference.

Figure 11.1 The Upload tool has become an option-rich feature with lots of choices.

Close Up with Mindy McNight

If you're not familiar with the Cute Girls Hairstyles website (http://www.cutegirlshairstyles.com) and the companion YouTube channel (http://www.youtube.com/cutegirlshairstyles), then prepare for a new experience. Mindy McNight started her blog in 2008 after getting constant requests from moms who all asked the same question: "How'd you do that hairstyle?" She has been listed as one of the top 50 women on YouTube and has built a thriving online business (see Figure 11.2).

Figure 11.2 The My Cute Girls Hairstyles YouTube channel art

■ Q. Tell us about your business—how did it start?

A. For many years, I would get stopped all the time when out shopping with my four daughters by moms wanting to know how I had created the girls' intricate hairstyles. As willing as I was to stop and explain, it became too much when some moms actually asked me to undo the hairstyle and redo it, or re-create it on their own daughters. As such, I began posting hairstyle tutorials via step-by-step photos on my blog at CuteGirlsHairstyles.com in October 2008. It was easier to refer them to a website than to spend so much time explaining . . . and I was finally able to get my shopping done without much interruption.

■ Q. When did you first envision using YouTube as part of your efforts?

A. During the next several months or so, fans began asking me for more pictures in the blog posts (to better show what happened between steps 4 and 5, for example). It quickly became too tedious for me to take so many still shots while completing the hairstyle, so I asked my husband to help. After another few months, even he grew tired of taking the photos and suggested that we use a USB Flip minicamera to film the hairstyle, upload it to YouTube, grab the embed code, and place it in the blog post rather than photos. That way, moms could start/stop/rewind/fast-forward/pause the video at any point to better understand the hairstyle.

Q. Did you have a large following off YouTube that you used to grow your YouTube results, or did you build a following on YouTube first?

A. We built a small base off YouTube first, which we know made a huge long-term contribution to our YouTube success. By the time we started using YouTube, our photo tutorial blog was generating approximately 1,500 page views per day. We would not classify that as large, but it did help jump-start our video view counts on YouTube. In those days on YouTube, if a video in a category reached a certain level of views in a short amount of time, your video would make the Most Watched list on YouTube (either daily, weekly, monthly, or all-time). Your video appearing on that list would generate new views, since that list was published in real time on YouTube. Making that list also placed a "badge" on your profile, further lending credence to your channel for new visitors who were more likely to subscribe by seeing those badges.

Q. Was there a tipping point where you realized YouTube was going to work well for you?

A. We felt that the average extra cash amount needed to dramatically reduce bankruptcy in the average U.S. hardworking and frugal home was around $400 per month. Once we hit that threshold, we were ecstatic and very grateful. In terms of what catapulted our success, it was when YouTube recognized CuteGirlsHairstyles' hard work and nominated us as one of four young channels for May 2011's "On the Rise" contest. This is a program where fans vote on their favorite over a two-week period of time, with the winner earning a feature on the YouTube home page for a day. We were privileged enough to win, and since then we have just been trying to keep our heads above water!

■ Q. How does your YouTube work compare with other social media or traffic-generating activities?

A. We take great care in making sure that our YouTube content is good and consistent and that the social engagement is there. However, it is important to never rely on only one social platform with your online business. We all learned that lesson when Facebook implemented its "Promoted Post" feature for pages, which greatly diluted the ability for fans who had liked our page to see our posts. We put so much effort and pocket cash into growing our Facebook fan base early on, and it was literally obliterated to less than 30 percent efficacy in driving traffic to our blog posts or YouTube videos. For that reason, we have used three social media platforms as a core, each strategically driving to the other, with additional social platforms ancillary to those. If one were to become less effective, we have another with a following right behind it. In the early years, it was our blog, Facebook, and YouTube. Today, it is our blog, Instagram, and YouTube. We also will never forget that it was due to our loyal blog fans, who were there from the beginning, that this

POWER TIP

Use a few strategic social media platforms as your core locations; then allow other sites to be ancillary. Never be dependent on just one online location for staying connected to your audience.

YouTube success began. For that reason, we make sure that CuteGirlsHairstyles.com has a great design, functionality, and SEO, which gives a "stickiness" factor for new and returning visitors.

▪ Q. What were some of your early challenges or struggles, and how did you overcome them?

A. We did not know that social media could earn money, nor that it would take so much time. I began and continue to do this out of sheer passion for hairstyles and the desire to help other moms find quality bonding time with their daughters every morning before school. I have to admit that about two years in, the demand by fans to create better hairstyles more often quickly overrode my passion and consumed so much of my time. I am a mom to six beautiful children, and with my husband, they are my first priority. About two years in, I decided that one hairstyle per week was all that I could do. I held to it, and I know that may have upset many fans at the time, but it worked for us; and that change in direction tempered the expectations of our fans, and they respected us for it.

▪ Q. What results or successes have you achieved because of YouTube?

A. For me, any success on YouTube will not compensate for failure as a mother. My goal is to raise my children with good morals, respect for others, and to be great contributors to society. More than any earnings or notoriety, the best reward for me is when young girls write in or comment that they are from broken homes, or that they have lost their mother, and they think of me as their "YouTube mom." Mothers often write to share how much they enjoy talking and bonding with their young daughters while re-creating one of my styles. Many young teenage girls who cannot afford cute name-brand clothes tell me that by wearing a cute hairstyle, many more girls at school talk to them, or that a specific crush commented on their hair. That is the most rewarding success for me.

■ **Q. If you were sitting down with someone just getting started on YouTube, what advice would you give the person?**

A. YouTube is the second largest search engine on the Internet (behind Google, which owns YouTube). Download the YouTube Playbook and read through it a few times. For us, the four most important YouTube tips are to create quality content, tag it the right way, upload on a consistent schedule, and engage with your fans. Beyond those, vlog for the passion and not for the money. If you are vlogging for the earnings, you will be sorely disappointed. Find what you love to do, something you are passionate about, and vlog it! The hardest step to take always appears to be the first one. Looking back, it was definitely the easiest!

■ **Q. What common mistakes do you see business owners making on YouTube?**

A. They look at the success of a channel or a brand and think that YouTube success is easily replicated, so they go all-in with expensive cameras and film crews, writers, etc. We started with a non-HD flip camera. Pretty much everyone has an HD camera today on his or her cell phone, and that is all that is needed to get started. Engagement is key. Many business owners think that getting the video view for the CPM or sale conversion is the end goal. Your end goal should be repeat viewers. Be yourself, and don't try to be someone you are not, because your fans will likely sense the lack of authenticity and never come back.

■ **Q. How has it changed your life and/or business for the better?**

A. YouTube is now part of our family. What we have learned has provided a skill set that will be valuable for years to come. Furthermore, we were able to pay for two adoptions and the needed home improvements and a new vehicle to accommodate them. We will forever be grateful to YouTube for creating a platform that would eventually provide the means for us to complete our family. If that isn't a change for the better, then I do not know what is!

■ Q. What are some of the most important techniques or tools you've discovered to help you grow your business with YouTube?

A. With so many millions of channels on the platform today, pretty much the most efficient way to grow a small channel is via collaborations with other channels that are similar in size. If we had done this early on, we would be more than double the size we are today! Don't forget to use YouTube's Annotation tool to help drive viewers to other videos and the Keyword Generator for relevant video tags. It is also very important to issue a call to action at the end of each video (such as "Be sure to subscribe" or "Follow us on Instagram").

■ Q. Can you distill your YouTube advice down into several key tips for readers?

A. Vlog because you have a passion for what you are doing, not for the revenue. Your videos are, in essence, a conversation with your viewers, so be authentic and engage your viewers. Even if you only end up with one subscriber, you may never know the difference you are making in that one individual's life. Take it from this YouTube mom—remember the "You" in YouTube and be yourself; that is why your parents love you in the first place!

And Action!

(1) Learn the process of uploading your first video to YouTube. (2) Determine if a Google Hangout webcam-captured video might be a good match for your efforts. (3) Learn to use the YouTube Keyword Suggestion Tool to ensure you tag your videos properly. (4) Learn the "cute girl" lessons and develop a core set of social media platforms that work together to reinforce engagement. (5) Be sure to make videos because of a love for the topic and a desire to help people.

Part 4

SOCIAL STRATEGIES ON YOUTUBE

YouTube: The Social Network

ake a random walk down Madison Avenue and ask the PR and marketing executives you see sipping on lattes to name the top social
networks. Easy, right? But a good percentage of them will fail to
mention YouTube. In a culture dominated by the craze of discovering,
reporting on, and documenting the growth of new social networks,
somehow YouTube has been shafted. My theory is that people who don't
personally use it for marketing don't see the social side of YouTube and
therefore fail to acknowledge it in this category. This "YouTube blindness" happens with journalists, bloggers, ad agency types, and (most
importantly for our discussion) marketing executives whom we are
competing against.

Easily Found Shocking Examples

Let me prove to you that people have YouTube blindness. I just Googled
"top social networks," and here is a summary of the organic search results. I have decided not to mention the names to protect the guilty, but
if you want, you can repeat this same experiment and see the specific
websites:

- The first Google result displays a list that doesn't include YouTube.
- The second result displays a list that doesn't include YouTube.

- The third result displays a list that doesn't include YouTube.

- The fourth result is a Wikipedia page that lists all major social networks alphabetically, but it doesn't include YouTube.

- The fifth result has a list that (finally) includes YouTube. Way to go http://www.webmediabistro.com!

- The sixth result displays a list that doesn't include YouTube.

- The seventh result is a list that includes YouTube. Way to go http://www.ZDNet.com!

- The eighth result is a list that does not include YouTube.

- The ninth and tenth results aren't relevant search results. One is an article about a company, and the other is a list of the top dating social networks.

Let's take our experiment a step further and audit these top-result providers to see whether they have YouTube channels. Here is the outcome:

- Site #1—no

- Site #2—yes (with 21 subscribers)

- Sites #3 and 4—No

- Site #5—Yes (with 3,372 subscribers and 2.5 million video views)

- Site #6—Yes (with just over 100,000 subscribers)

- Site #7—yes (with 4,625 subscribers)

- Site #8—no

- Sites # 9 and 10 n/a

Can you see the correlation? The sites that reported that YouTube is a social network (sites #5 and #7) both have a solid YouTube marketing presence. Only two of the six sites that reported that YouTube is not a social network have a marketing presence on the platform, and one of those has a presence that is almost completely insignificant.

You may have noticed that there is one exception. Search result #6 did not list YouTube as a social network, and yet it has a dynamic and huge YouTube audience. Odd, right? Well, the explanation is simple. It allows a lot of guest posts, and the post that ranked well for "top social networks" was written by someone who didn't include YouTube. I'd imagine that if one of the company executives had written the article, it would have been on the list.

So my point with all this quick and dirty research is simple: only a fraction of our "well-informed" Internet authors and content creators managing these (very large) websites consider YouTube to be a social network. They have YouTube blindness. So when you show up on YouTube, you might ask the question, where have all the marketers gone? To Facebook, I guess.

In the Land of the Blind, the One-Eyed Man Is King

If you're like me, when you see a strong pattern like this, rather than thinking, "Maybe I'm wrong and need to change my view," you think, "Sweet—I can exploit this to my advantage." And sure enough, you can. You can jump into it, and chances are, your competitors will be absent.

The fact that YouTube is the third most visited website on the planet behind Facebook and Google (according to the Alexa Top 500 Global Sites report) means that you have a massive pool of people hanging out on the site, and marketers are missing in action. I know—this is another huge claim I'm making. But look at your niche or industry and ask the question, are the market leaders using YouTube effectively? The answer may very well be no. So even if you feel small, wimpy, and unsure of yourself, jump into it anyway. Even if you think you cannot produce videos that will win any Oscars, don't overestimate the competition. The old adage is certainly true—"In the land of the blind, the one-eyed man is king."

Our Head-to-Head Comparison

In Chapter 3, we talked about the challenges big companies face and how small guerrilla marketers can outperform their much larger rivals. To prove my point, I'll use our small business and the niche we operate in as an example. Don't worry; I'm not trying to sell you doll clothes. But the exploration of this niche will give you some insight into how to look at your industry competitors.

We started our business in February 2008 as a microscopic competitor in the American Girl doll category. We sold $12,000 in product our first year. Pleasant Rowland, an educator and entrepreneur, created the American Girl doll category in 1986. According to Wikipedia, she sold the company to Mattel for $700 million in 1998. The brand reached $350 million in sales in 2001 and is second in the doll category behind Barbie, which Mattel also owns. It is truly a massive brand that dominates its category. Truth is, there is no real competition.

So the American Girl Doll Company is our primary competitor. We consider ourselves the second leading brand in this category, although I'm not sure anyone else would see it that way. And the category is so far off the beaten path that there are no industry analysts or commentators except for a few bloggers. As most guerrilla marketers would do in our situation, we work hard to avoid head-to-head product competition, and instead we try to add unique value to enhance and expand the ecosystem that Mattel has created. We consider our work complementary and supportive of Mattel's amazing ecosystem.

So it stands to reason that when we look at American Girl's YouTube marketing strategy, we would be at a distinct disadvantage. Mattel, after all, has the moviemaking production system that has created scores of films of every type—live-action films (shown in theaters), direct-to-video projects, and TV movies. You'd think that when it comes to YouTube, we're toast. But as we look at the two YouTube channels side by side, it's an outcome that might surprise you. These are the stats as of Sunday morning, June 23, 2013:

	Liberty Jane Clothing	American Girl Doll Company
Channel	youtube.com /libertyjaneclothing	youtube.com /AmericanGirl
Videos	250+	26
Subscribers	10,460	9,449
Video Views	1,925,564	1,206,055
Joined	January 2008	March 2006

Even though we joined almost two years after American Girl did, we have 10,460 subscribers compared with its 9,449. We have 1.9 million video views compared with its 1.2 million. And again, we run our business from our back patio (in the summer) and from our kitchen table (in the winter), and Mattel is a multibillion dollar corporation.

These comparisons are neither a criticism of American Girl's work nor an attempt to glorify our work. They're simply illustrative of my point: large corporations have a harder time ramping up on YouTube than small guerrilla marketers do. YouTube is a weird and wild place where big companies are frequently hindered and tiny start-ups are frequently supercharged.

Can you see how we're beating the folks at American Girl? It's completely obvious, isn't it? We've published 10 times as many videos as they have. We've published over 250 compared with their 26. We are willing to turn on our iPhone 5 and record a new video right here, right now. Whereas, and I'm just guessing here, for them to publish a new video, it would probably be a massive corporate undertaking with many approval levels, budget implications, staffing issues, and legal matters to resolve years in advance. They are forced to go with a quality-over-quantity approach that safeguards their brand. That is completely rational and wise. We can take the opposite approach and go with a quantity-over-quality approach that takes advantage of our small size.

> **POWER TIP**
>
> Publish more frequently that your competition. Like more videos than your competition. Have more conversations on YouTube than your competition. Sometimes success is as simple as logging as much time on the site as you can.

There is another aspect of American Girl's YouTube work that you wouldn't notice unless you looked closely. The company has disabled the conversation (aka channel comments) functionality. I'm guessing the rationale is that the American Girl team does not want YouTube to be a place where customer service issues are posted or complaints are vented.

When you're a large brand, keeping your channel comments off is a sensible approach to YouTube. I'd do the same thing. We, on the other hand, are desperate to engage with prospective customers on YouTube, and we are willing to deal with the awkwardness of customer service complaints, angry customers, and vocal critics for the chance of having a conversation.

We are so small, that if I see a complaint on our YouTube channel, I just lean over and ask Cinnamon (our lead designer) about the issue; she tells me about it, and I respond under our account name. Bam! The two cofounders have personally handled a customer service issue. This type of quick and informal response frequently shocks our YouTube visitors. They act as if it is the most incredible thing they've ever seen. They don't realize how small our operation really is.

Look at your primary competitors or industry leaders and see where you stand compared with them. You'll likely find that YouTube provides a distinct advantage to the little guys if the little guys are willing to create a YouTube marketing strategy. You'll also immediately see things that they are not doing that you could do, gaps and holes in their strategy that you can easily fill.

Seven Smart Social Activities on YouTube

Now that we've established the fact that YouTube is a social network and have expanded on the idea that the little guys can compete effectively even against much larger competitors, let's look at the social activities that can really jump-start your YouTube marketing strategy.

1. Post Videos

Sometimes the most obvious action is the wisest. You cannot grow a large subscribership on YouTube if you're not regularly publishing video content. Each time you publish a video, it is included in your feed, and your subscribers can engage with your work. When they do, their subscribers see the interaction. It stands to reason that the more you post, the more your subscribers will engage with a video, and the more you'll be discovered. The other reason to post frequently is to ensure that you have videos that appear when people search for the keywords related to your industry.

2. Comment on Videos

There are most likely countless videos to comment on in your niche or industry. You can comment on your customers' videos, competitors' videos, and industry-related peers' videos. When you comment wisely, you share your encouragement, wisdom, and insight. You establish yourself as an authority in your niche or industry.

3. Like Videos

On YouTube, you can give a video a thumbs-up or a thumbs-down. Liking videos is a sign of support and encouragement to the video maker. It is probably the simplest social action on YouTube, and it will only take a split second.

4. Add a Video to a Playlist

If you consider yourself a curator of information and education for your prospects, then creating playlists that go beyond your own videos makes a lot of sense. And when you add a video to a playlist, you affirm and encourage the video maker.

5. Make a Channel Comment

When you comment on a channel that belongs to one of your customers, prospects, or industry experts, you make yourself known to the person in a friendly and engaging way.

6. Subscribe to Another User

Subscribing is the biggest form of support you can provide on YouTube. Subscribing is voting.

7. Send a Bulletin

We'll talk more about this in the chapter on traffic strategies, but you can send a message straight to the feed of every one of your subscribers. This is an incredibly powerful marketing tool.

Troubleshooting Social Challenges

Even if you're a small business, there are legitimate reasons to avoid being social on YouTube. But we strongly believe that the positives outweigh the negatives. Marketing managers might consider the following roadblocks particularly challenging.

Product Complaints

If your product is advertised via a video on YouTube, then prepare to have product complaints listed in the comments. Given the nature of consumers, even great products will provoke complaints and criticism. "My t-shirt arrived wrinkled." "My order was late." "I didn't expect this to smell like plastic." On and on. It's a hassle.

Pricing Complaints

One particular form of social commentary is more challenging than others, and that is pricing complaints. "I just bought it yesterday, and now it's on sale; can I get the discount mailed to me?" "You can buy the exact same thing for $10 less at Target." The price complaint is awkward to answer. It frequently takes time and energy and leaves you wondering why you're in business. But you've got to address these concerns if you have YouTube comments enabled.

Unwanted Brand or Positioning Advice

Complaints are one thing, but unwelcomed branding or positioning advice is almost worse. "You guys should give up competing against XYZ Company." "Your logo is dumb." Unfortunately, when customers get negative or cynical, they also get empowered to preach at you.

Unwanted Product Advice

Having your fans or customers make comments about your products can get very tiring. "You guys should really make this black." "Your product would be better if you had less buttons." "Using a zipper in the back is a bad way to design this product." Although it's almost always the case that customers don't know what they want until they see it, once they've seen it, they can think of a million ways you should have made it differently.

Unwanted Pricing Advice

The most common criticism we deal with on our YouTube channel is, "Your products are too expensive." If you're trying to roll out and maintain an ultrapremium pricing structure in your niche, then get ready to hear these comments.

In our niche, clothes for the American Girl doll line, the category leader is positioned as a high-price provider. We've positioned ourselves as the "ultrapremium" provider and sell our products for substantially more than American Girl does. It's a good place to be in the market, but you get this constant friction. Customers have the anchor in their mind of the category leader's prices. That anchor is a powerful psychological barrier to overcome. Needless to say, arguing the merits of an ultrapremium pricing strategy with your customers on YouTube is not a productive use of your time.

And Action!

(1) Decide to use YouTube as a social network. (2) Audit your niche or industry and see how you stack up compared with your competition. (3) Evaluate how you can fill a gap that is not being provided and do video that is more compelling or engaging in some way. (4) If all else fails, simply commit to publishing more videos than anyone else. Doing a weekly video is a solid goal. (5) Jump into the seven smart social media actions on YouTube and begin to make connections. (6) Prepare for trouble if you allow channel comments. We believe you should do it, but be ready to answer hard questions and moderate your channel regularly to ensure that customers get answers.

The Grand Opening of Your Shiny New YouTube Attraction

Last month, my wife and I and our three kids took a family trip to Disneyland in Anaheim and spent several days wandering the parks and having a great time together. It was the first time we had been there in eight years, so our anticipation was high.

As you might guess, I was assigned the fatherly duty of sitting down for three hours to reserve our seats for the Fantasmic Light Show while my family ran wild. Been there? So there I sat at the River Belle Terrace, pondering life, overeating, updating my Instagram and Facebook accounts, checking my e-mail, and thinking about this book. And, of course, repeating the statement, "Yeah, these seats are taken."

Your YouTube Theme Park

As I sat there, the thought occurred to me—our little company's social media channels are like attractions in our version of an online theme park. Can you tell I was bored? Anyway, the idea was simple. Like Disneyland, you can have different spaces and places that are designed to do different things. If you do social media right, then you can weave a whole collection of exciting activities together to make a really memorable experience for your prospects and customers.

> **POWER TIP**
>
> Treat your social media channels like the various attractions
> at an online theme park. Strive to engage in different ways
> on different platforms, and in that way give your prospects
> and customers a fun and memorable experience.

What elements can you create via social media? Let's consider a few of them and how you might pull them off.

Games

Games are one of the best attractions in your social media theme park. People love to have fun and engage with your brand in a trivial manner. And just having a game will position you as a fun and lighthearted person. People like to be your favorite fan and consider themselves an expert on your business. What kind of games can you have? They don't have to be overly complicated or tech savvy. No programmers from Eastern Europe are required. Just find enjoyable and engaging ways to involve people. Trivia questions are one good example. At Liberty Jane Clothing, we do Trivia Thursday via our Facebook fan page. Cammie, our Facebook coordinator, simply asks questions about our brand, our products, or our niche. There is no prize and technically no winner; it's just a way to connect with people.

Contests

Social contests are a great way to engage your prospects and customers. We'll talk more about our work with YouTube contests in an upcoming chapter. This has been our social media highlight for the last five years. It's our version of Fantasmic—where we pull out all the stops and try to put on an incredible show for our fans and followers.

Entertaining Performances That Educate

As we discussed in earlier chapters, your tutorials or how-to videos can be a great way to entertain and educate as you show your prospects how something is done. At Liberty Jane, we do Tutorial Tuesday. We launch this out onto our Facebook fan page, but the links drive people to our Pinterest tutorial board. The beauty of this method is that it helps to cross-pollinate our Facebook followers with our Pinterest profile with the hope of having them join us on that platform. The tutorials we feature aren't even our own work, necessarily. They are just related to our niche or category.

Behind-the-Scenes Tours

We regularly use our YouTube videos, as well as our Instagram and Pinterest profiles, to give people a behind-the-scenes look at our work. From shooting videos in our office, to creating Pinterest pinboards entitled, "Projects I'm Working On," we try to reveal behind-the-scenes information as much as we can. The only thing we don't do is tweet about our activities. We've just never gotten into Twitter and feel like it's too labor-intensive to maintain. But maybe it's a good match for you.

Shopping

Have you ever noticed how much you spend at Disneyland? When I was a kid, the exit to each ride didn't deposit you into the middle of a store, with branded apparel, but now that seems to be the approach. Can you blame Disney? I can't. The real question is, can you deposit your fans and followers into your store at the end of each social media activity? And can you do it in a way that doesn't feel salesy or smarmy? Can you do it in a way that seems helpful, low key, and exciting?

Memorable Characters

Great brands produce iconic characters that play an important role. They serve as the human side of the business. A great character associated with your brand can welcome people, explain things, instruct and educate, and provide comic relief. Memorable characters can be you, your coworkers or employees, celebrity spokespeople, or a spokesperson whom you turn into a celebrity. As we've mentioned, we started by having our young daughter serve as the official "spokesgirl." Can you do the same or something similar?

Memorable characters don't have to be real people, of course—they can be completely fictional or even a pet dog. When people bond with your unique and memorable characters, they are bonding with your brand.

Drama and Excitement

No good theme park can exist without having a sense of drama and excitement. Your social media business is the same. The simplest way to have drama and excitement is to have a special sales event or annual activity that you drive toward all year long. For our work, that is our eBay auctions. We feature them on all our social media channels and in particular use YouTube to display the product videos.

Fan Photos

One of your best pieces of content for social sharing is fan-generated photos. You can use several social channels to curate this content. At Liberty Jane, we ask for it every Friday with our Fan Friday post. We simply ask our Facebook followers to post their photos of our products on our fan page every Friday. You can organize these into an album on your Facebook fan page, or you can keep them on a pinboard on Pinterest.

Fan Videos

On one occasion, we noticed that one of our young customers had created a video where she opened her Liberty Jane package slowly, describing each step in detail and with a lot of energy and enthusiasm. It was her way of sharing the experience with her friends on YouTube. The video was popular, and we realized that if we'd promote it and talk about it, it might start happening regularly. So we blogged about it, included it in our e-mail newsletter, and posted it on our Facebook fan page. Our tactic worked. Now we regularly see fan videos that are similar. We do our best to feature them, comment on them, and share them. We also collect them on our Pinterest account. You can see them at http://pinterest.com/cinnamonmiles/seen-wearing-liberty-jane/.

Get People Moving from One Attraction to the Next

There are great reasons to integrate YouTube into your social media mix. The better you integrate your social media channels, the more your followers will migrate from one of your social media channels to others. And that's a good thing. You want to create multiple points of connection so that people encounter your brand in various ways. If the only connection point is YouTube and they stop using YouTube, then you've lost your opportunity to influence them. You want multiple points of connection so your brand is always conveniently on your prospects' radar.

There are lots of creative ways to integrate YouTube into your social media efforts. Remember that your goal, like Disneyland's goal, is to get people migrating from one activity to the next. Let's review a few of the easiest and best ways to do this.

Publish Unique Content on Various Sites

The easiest way to get people to move from being a fan on one social channel to another social channel is to offer unique things on each channel. Have you ever been at Disneyland by Thunder Mountain Railroad and had one of your kids say, "The only thing I want to do today is go on the new Cars Land ride in California Adventure." It's a hassle, but you know what you have to do. Start walking and make your way toward that attraction. In the same way, you want to offer unique activities and engagement on various social media channels and not on the others. This forces people to join you on more than one platform if they want the "full experience." This might seem counterintuitive, but by announcing on Twitter, YouTube, Facebook, LinkedIn, and Pinterest that we document and share our behind-the-scenes projects on our Instagram account, those people will know that if they want to experience the behind-the-scenes "ride," then they have to migrate to Instagram-Land. It's that simple. You can coordinate this type of game plan for each social media platform you're on.

Run a Contest on One; Advertise It on Another

Your YouTube content can play nicely on your Facebook fan page. That's an easy integration activity. Simply copy the YouTube video URL and share it in a Facebook post. The video will play directly in Facebook, and people can click through to visit your YouTube channel. But you shouldn't share all your videos, as mentioned above. So how do you take advantage of this opportunity? You can create a fun contest on YouTube (more on that in an upcoming chapter) or even Pinterest; then share it on Facebook, Twitter, and Instagram. This forces your non-YouTube users to get into YouTube and engage with you there if they want to win the prize.

Use Your YouTube Videos in Your E-mails

Your e-mail list is your first and best social media tool. It's easy to include a link to a YouTube video in your e-mail. You can simply explain your new video and add a link to it. To take it a step further and really improve your click-through rate, take a screenshot image of your video; then include that in your e-mail and link the image to the YouTube video. That way, when people click the image of the video, they are taken to your channel where it begins playing. Make sure the screenshot image includes the triangle "play" icon, so people know it is a playable video, not just a picture. Remember, e-mail is the original and best social media marketing method.

Make Unique Collections on Pinterest

Pinterest allows you to curate content in a fun and interesting way. You can curate your own content so that it integrates your social media work. For example, create a "Behind-the-Scenes" board on Pinterest. Include content from behind-the-scenes videos you've made and kept on YouTube, behind-the-scenes pictures (and video) you've taken from Instagram, and screenshots from behind-the-scenes tweets from your Twitter account. Then promote this special board in your e-mail newsletter. You'll have effectively exposed people to your YouTube, Instagram, and Twitter activities.

Run Coupons and Special Offers on Just One Site

The simplest way to get people to move from one platform to the next is to offer an incentive. Common incentives are coupons, special offers, or free (digital) products. If you offer a 10 percent off coupon on Twitter, then your Twitter followers will see it, but your followers on YouTube won't. So why not make a brief video on YouTube and say, "Hey, this week we're going to publish a coupon on our Twitter feed. It will be a 24-hour special, so be sure to follow us on Twitter if you don't already." You could also do this on Instagram by recording a 15-second video clip. In that way, your YouTube and Instagram followers are encouraged to follow you on Twitter if they want the coupon.

Close Up with Rosanna Pansino

Actress Rosanna Pansino combines a successful acting career with her YouTube channel efforts (see Figure 13.1). She's been on top TV shows like *Parks and Recreation*, *CSI*, and *Glee*. She also hosts *Nerdy Nummies* on her YouTube channel, where she's grown an audience of over 750,000 subscribers and 135 million video views. You can see her work on YouTube at http://www.youtube.com/user/RosannaPansino. We asked Ro to tell us about her YouTube work and how she's grown her following so well.

Figure 13.1 The Rosanna Pansino YouTube channel art

■ **Q. Tell us about your business—how did it start?**

A. My YouTube channel primarily focuses on my geeky themed baking show called *Nerdy Nummies*. For the future, I am also working on other projects such as a web series, vlogs, original music, gaming, and even a movie. I originally started using YouTube as a way to learn more about the video editing process as well as to have a place to be creative. I have also always enjoyed baking growing up, and shortly after starting my channel, decided to make a geeky baking show. At that time, there were no other geek culture, food-related shows out there, and I wanted to be the first. Jump forward a year or two, and here I am.

■ **Q. When did you first envision using YouTube as part of your efforts?**

A. Many of the people and friends I had grown close to in Los Angeles were either creating content full-time on YouTube already or working closely with those who do. I was able to draw a direct comparison with my traditional acting career and new media, as I was able to see both sides equally. As time went on, I really enjoyed being able to create my own content as well as still being able to take part in other people's projects.

■ **Q. Did you have a large following off YouTube that you used to grow your YouTube results, or did you build a following on YouTube first?**

A. Before starting YouTube, I had used websites like Facebook and Twitter to grow a small following. I had a much smaller following then than I do now, and the majority of people who watch my show found it through YouTube first. Some well-known people will grow their followings on these social websites before attempting to create video content online; it all just depends on their individual circumstances.

■ **Q. How does your YouTube work compare with other social media or traffic-generating activities?**

A. YouTube is a lot different from other traffic-generating activities in that you really have to create something interesting and engaging for people to want to see it. It has much more of a "community" feel than what you might find on other websites. To me, YouTube feels a lot more personal because viewers have direct communication with the content producer.

■ **Q. What were some of your early challenges or struggles, and how did you overcome them?**

A. The earliest struggle for me on YouTube was figuring out what to do and how to do it. I originally stepped into it with minimal experience in running a camera and editing a video. Once I had the basics figured out, I had to also decide what to do that people would find interesting.

■ **Q. What results or successes have you achieved because of YouTube?**

A. YouTube has allowed me to meet a lot of really cool and hardworking people whom I would have never been able to otherwise. The experience and constantly changing environment of online entertainment has accelerated my learning of all things digital.

■ **Q. If you were sitting down with someone just getting started with YouTube, what advice would you give?**

A. I think the best piece of advice that I could give to someone just starting out on YouTube is to be patient; it can take years to slowly build a following. While making online content can be extremely fun and rewarding, it also takes a lot of time. Even a video that may only be a couple minutes long can easily take a week or two to plan for. I would also recommend trying out different things until you find what fits your interests and personality best.

■ **Q. What common mistakes do you see business owners making on YouTube?**

A. I think one of the most common mistakes I see business owners make is that they completely undervalue YouTube as a legitimate platform. Many companies will make a couple of videos and then give up because they did not see immediate results. Making online content is a long-term investment and should be treated as such.

■ **Q. How has it changed your life and/or business for the better?**

A. YouTube has allowed me to do what I love more often and has given me the freedom to decide what I do day to day. It has given me opportunities to do things ranging all the way from hosting a cooking show to being a main character in an animated series. On top of that, I can work on the projects I want to work on instead of hoping the right one will present itself on its own. I also am able to communicate with my viewers much more directly and watch how I influence their lives on a much more personal level.

■ **Q. What are some of the most important techniques or tools you've discovered to help you grow your business on YouTube?**

A. In my opinion, the most important tool to grow your You-Tube channel is collaboration. Reaching out to others who are doing similar things can go a long way in establishing yourself.

■ **Q. Can you distill your YouTube advice down into several key tips for readers?**

A. 1. Have fun.

    2. Work hard.

    3. Collaborate with others.

    4. Take feedback and criticism.

    5. Interact with your followers.

    6. Keep at it for the long haul.

There is no one way to go about growing a following on YouTube, and all the top talent have gotten to where they are in different ways. What's most important is to just jump in with an open mind and learn from all your experiences.

And Action!

(1) Make it your goal to get your fans and followers migrating from one social media platform to the next so their bonds with you become stronger. (2) Come up with unique uses for your social media accounts so that if people want to experience everything you're doing, they'll have to join you on multiple platforms. (3) Identify offers and incentives you can use on one social media channel as motivation for people to join you on that channel. (4) Tell people what you're doing so they know the benefits of following you on multiple channels. (5) Find ways to collaborate to grow your followers.

YouTube Contests That Rock

R unning a contest on YouTube is an incredibly powerful way to connect with prospects within your niche or industry. Contests are
not difficult to run, they offer a very effective viral marketing tool,
and they give your fans and followers a unique, memorable experience.

We already discussed in an earlier chapter how most marketers
aren't on YouTube, and we noted that only a very small percentage of
those who are on YouTube will ever try to conduct a contest. So if you're
looking for an easy way to be memorable and bond with your prospects,
this is it. Chances are very good that no one in your niche or industry
has ever done a YouTube contest. Therefore, no prospect in your niche
or industry has ever been marketed to in this way. How rare is that? As
the Good Book says, the fields are white unto harvest.

In this chapter, we'll walk through how we do YouTube contests at
Liberty Jane Clothing. Our experience with contests on YouTube goes
back to the fall of 2008, when we created our first design contest. It got
people's attention, and they seemed to really enjoy it. We had hundreds
of responses, which shocked us. The video is still on YouTube in our
contests playlist, and you can watch it to see exactly how we did it. The
script was simple. The basic idea went something like this: "Design an
outfit for your doll; then make a video telling us all about it and place it
on YouTube as a response to this video. The winner will get the outfit—
made for free." My wife would look at the entries and pick one that she

knew she could make, and then we'd choose that as the winning design. This simple idea leverages our unique ability to design, as well as the entrant's imagination, to create a completely unique prize.

Because it was successful, we knew we had a new method of engaging with our audience. So we started to run the same type of contest twice a year. We don't really change anything. The rules, the prize, the method of entry—they're all the same each time. We have done this almost without fail for the last five years. It wasn't until the fall of 2013 that we had to adapt our plan slightly, as YouTube eliminated the video-response functionality. Moving forward we plan to use hashtags and playlists instead of video responses.

Our result? If you look at the third-party website http://vidstatsx .com/most-responded-how-to-style-videos-all-time, you'll see that Liberty Jane Clothing has 5 of the top 50 most-responded-to videos of all time in YouTube's "Howto & Style" category. Yes, "Most Responded Videos All Time" is a category. YouTube used to feature it more prominently, but now you have to look at third-party sites to see those lists. You can see the most-responded-to videos for a week, month, year, or all time. While new video responses cannot be added, you can still see the video responses added before August of 2013. It's incredibly uncommon to have a video make the list, and garnering a full 10 percent of the results is unheard of. You can find the most-viewed videos as well. How uncommon is it to get 5 out of the top 50 videos? Let's look at another example by way of comparison and as a cautionary tale.

At the same time we launched our first contest, a giant in the fashion industry launched a contest on his YouTube channel. I won't mention his name because his result was embarrassing, but he's an iconic designer from New York. His contest got only five entries, and all of them were off-topic spam responses. What did he do wrong? His video was shot in his studio, and he was speaking directly into the camera. So far so good, right? But his script went something like this: "Hey, YouTube, I want to see what you can design, so make a design and record a video describing what you made and save it as a response to this video. I'll choose the winner and talk about your design. So go ahead, what are you waiting for?" Can you imagine that? "I'll . . . talk about your design"—that was the reward. No trip to New York. No design apprenticeship. No introduction to the fashion A-list. No front-row seat at the next runway show. No shopping spree. Nothing. Not even an "I'll make your outfit for you for free." His failure points out a vital requirement—your contest needs to motivate action with a clear and compelling prize.

By contrast, our top contest resulted in over 2,400 unique video responses. You might be thinking, "Yeah, and they're all 13-year-old girls who can never purchase your products." But you'd be wrong. We regularly get adults who enter the contests. And even more frequently, we get moms and daughters entering together as a family project. What could be better for a mom and daughter than bonding over a Liberty Jane Clothing contest? I can't think of anything, except maybe shopping on one of our websites.

Like all marketing activities, contests can be done well or done badly. But the quality needed isn't about flawless videography; it's about offering something of value and a good time. Think about offering a reward that integrates these ideas:

1. Leverage your company's unique skills and talents. Can you create a completely custom product or service experience as a prize? If you have unique design talent, use it.

2. Can you turn your normal product into a one-of-a-kind collector's item as your prize? If you can't make something special, then maybe you can give away "the first copy of our new product—signed by the team."

3. Give people inside access or a custom learning experience. Can you offer the winner of your contest a two-day internship at your office? If you work at a casino, that would probably be a hit. If you work at the county jail, it probably wouldn't.

4. What about being a guest of honor at a national trade show or convention? Could you offer the winner an all-expense-paid trip to your industry's convention of the year?

5. Can you allow someone to be an "official brand ambassador"? More on that idea in a moment.

6. Can you give away a complete collection of your products? If all else fails, can you simply give a way a really nice collection of your products or services?

But Will Your Prospects Make Videos?

Who do you think will most likely make a video as an entry to a contest? Probably a young person, right? While that's not universally true, you do need to think about whether your followers are going to make a video. If your target market is seniors in high school, you're probably fine. If they're senior citizens, then you might have a hard time getting people to enter. In fact, there are a whole set of things to consider before deciding on a contest, including the following:

- **Will your prospective customers make a YouTube video?** Some types of consumers are more inclined to make videos than others. If you haven't seen any evidence that your core audience is willing to make videos and put them on YouTube, then chances are they won't. Don't try to tilt at windmills and reshape the behavior of the masses. If a video contest won't work, then consider doing a different type of contest, like a blog comment contest or a pin-it-to-win-it contest on Pinterest.

- **How passionate are people about your brand?** You might be a marketer at a giant company, but that doesn't mean people have a giant amount of love for your brand. If you have neutral or negative brand sentiment, then a contest might not be a good idea.

- **How well known is your brand in your niche?** If your product is good, but very few people have heard about you nationally, then it might be a challenge to get them to enter your contest. In these cases in particular, your prize must be clear and compelling.

- **Is your prize something that will get people highly motivated?** You can have a much-loved brand and a good followership on YouTube, but if you create a contest with a prize that doesn't resonate with people, then your response could be flat.

Could You Benefit from Entering a Contest?

Let's take a small detour for a moment and look at contests from a different perspective; then we'll get back to how to effectively run your contest. Let's look at a fun question: Are there contests that you could enter that would substantially boost your credibility, business success, or prestige? Chances are, the answer is yes. Take the time to spot them and enter. What do you have to lose? And if your video work is good, then your chances are probably above average. Let me mention our best example.

We were less than two years into launching our small business, and my cofounder and wife, Cinnamon, spotted a golden opportunity on YouTube. It was a contest put on by Bernina, one of the world's leading sewing machine makers. What was the prize? Win the contest and you could become "an official brand ambassador for Bernina and receive one of their sewing machines." What were the official duties of a brand ambassador? We had no idea. But we knew that if Cinnamon could add that prestigious credential to her "About us" description, then it would give her a lot of credibility as a seamstress.

As it turned out, there weren't very many entries. Apparently not too many people had a deep desire to be an official brand ambassador for Bernina. I'm not sure why—it sounded spectacular to us and still does. Cinnamon won, and for more than three years now, she's had an ongoing relationship with the company. We continue to believe that her biography is enhanced nicely by that third-party endorsement. What was the benefit for Bernina? Well, we've had 300,000 digital patterns downloaded from our website over the last three years, and the vast majority show a Bernina sewing machine. We assume Bernina is very happy with that level of free product placement.

You might find a contest that gives you any one of the following benefits, and if you do, you should enter:

- A unique title or designation

- A formal role with a company

- A free product or service that offsets expenses

- Prestige or credibility

- Cash

- A relationship with someone whom you want to work with

> **POWER TIP**
>
> Look for contests that you can enter that will boost your business in a meaningful way. Think about why you want to enter and the types of rewards that motivate you as a prospective entrant. Take those lessons and apply them to your contests.

Complying with YouTube Contest Guidelines

Not all social media sites allow contests to be run on their platforms. We are lucky that YouTube allows them. But you need to understand the limits and guidelines. You can find the official YouTube guidelines for contests at http://bit.ly/1afX2vw. Here are the 10 general restrictions and requirements according to the March 15, 2013, version of the policy:

1. You are solely responsible for your contest.

2. Your contest on YouTube must comply with all applicable federal, state and local laws, rules, and regulations in the jurisdiction(s) where your contest is offered or promoted.

3. Your contest cannot infringe upon or encourage the infringement of any third-party rights or the participation in any unlawful activity.

4. Your contest may only accept entries from users aged 18 and up, or, the age of the majority in the jurisdiction(s) where your contest is offered or promoted if it is over 18.

5. You cannot ask the users to give all rights for, or transfer the ownership of, their entry to you.

6. Your contest must be free to enter.

7. Your contest must be a game of skill where the winner is determined by a set of clear judging criteria.

8. You may not utilize channel functions, such as video likes or view counts, to conduct your contest.

9. You may only use any data collected from entrants for contest administration purposes and cannot re-use the data for marketing purposes (even if the user has expressly opted-in to that use).

10. You cannot use the YouTube embedded player or YouTube API to run a contest offsite.

Additionally, YouTube requires every contest to have official rules. Here are the requirements related to rules, according to the March 15, 2013, version of the policy:

1. You must have a set of official rules, which:

   a. Include links to the YouTube Terms of Service and Community Guidelines. You must also state that "entries which don't comply will be disqualified."

   b. State all disclosures required by all applicable federal, state and local laws, rules and regulations in the jurisdiction in which your contest is offered or promoted.

   c. Are wholly compliant and consistent with the YouTube Terms of Service.

2. Your contest must be conducted, and all prizes awarded as outlined in your rules.

3. You are responsible for your rules and all aspects of your contest administration.

4. Your rules must clearly state that YouTube is not a sponsor of your contest and ask users to release YouTube from all liability related to your contest.

5. You must include a legally compliant privacy notice in your Official Rules which explains how you will use any personal data you collect for the contest and adhere to that use.

Again, you should read the official YouTube guidelines for contests at http://bit.ly/1afX2vw. There are additional sections that I did not include in this brief summary, including your responsibilities and liability. You certainly don't want to run afoul of Google Inc.

Only Use a Skills-Based Contest

You may have noticed the statement, "Your contest must be a game of skill." Based on our humble research efforts, we've identified three types of potential "games" that you can set up online, and only one of them is appropriate for YouTube. Let's review them briefly:

- **A skills-based contest.** In a "game of skill" or a "skills-based contest," you use a set of criteria objectively to choose a winner. Maybe it's drawing or design talent. Maybe it's vocal talent. Maybe it's programming talent. Whatever. They are your criteria, so obviously you get to interpret them, but they must be clearly explained so that participants know what skill you are judging them on. The criteria should be explained in your video, as well as in your official rules.

- **A drawing.** A drawing is simply focused on getting people to enter; then a winner is randomly chosen without the objective criteria of a skill or talent being evaluated in the decision-making process. This type of game is not permitted on YouTube.

- **An illegal lottery.** If you require people to pay to enter your contest, then you may be setting up a lottery. And most states have specific laws to ensure that you can't do this without serious fines and legal trouble. Again, YouTube doesn't permit this type of game.

Basic Steps to a Good Contest

Skills-based contests aren't overly burdensome to administrate. If you get 2,400 entries, then you'll have a lot of videos to watch. But until then, it won't be too bad. Let's review the simple steps involved in running an effective contest:

1. Produce a contest launch video that is scripted so it is both fun and very clear about the rules and process.

2. Write the official rules and place them on your blog or website. Then in the launch video, mention the location of the official rules and also include a link to the URL in your video's description

information. That way, people can easily find the link to the official rules.

3. Have a precise start date and end date. We usually let our contests run for four weeks. After the contest is over, modify the title of the video in YouTube to include "ended," as in "Fall 2013 Design Contest—ENDED," so people know not to apply.

4. Explain the judging criteria so people know what type of entry you're looking for.

5. Explain the video guidelines in clear terms so people know what type of video to make to enter the contest. Guidelines such as "between one minute and three minutes long," "hold the camera very still," and "make sure your video is shot in good lighting so we can see the entry" are all good pointers.

6. Clearly announce the prize and any second- or third-place prizes as well.

7. Explain how people are supposed to enter. Before August 2013 the common method of entry was to simply ask people to "Make a video and add it as a response to this video." An alternate way to ask people to enter is to use a specific hashtag in the title, such as #LJCFall2013Contest.

8. Make sure your contest is fun. If you come across as a jerk or as someone who is overly critical or judgmental, then no one will want to enter.

9. During the contest period, monitor your contest and report any video entries that are spam.

10. After the entry period is over, start to watch all the video entries and determine your top finalists. Contact your prizewinners and ask them to confirm that they are eligible to enter according to the rules, and let them know that you need their address so that you can send the prize. Give them a due date to reply back and inform them that if you don't hear from them, you'll be forced to choose another winner. Ask them to keep your conversation strictly confidential until the results video is published.

11. You don't need to do this, but people like to know how well they did in the contest. So it is our practice to place the top 50 videos in a playlist, with the top 10 in rank order. We call it something like "Fall 2013 Design Contest Top 50 Results Playlist." The first video in the playlist is the grand prize winner and so on. We keep this playlist private until after we launch our results video; then we make it public.

12. Make a results video where you thank everyone for entering. We like to count down the top 10 finalists and then announce the winner with a lot of hype and energy.

13. Send your winners their prizes.

And Action!

(1) Consider whether you could motivate your prospects to enter a YouTube contest by promising an adequately cool prize. (2) Look for contests that you could enter to boost your business results. (3) Consider the types of prizes you could give away that would blow people's minds and get them very energized to enter. (4) Read the official YouTube contest policies and guidelines. (5) Design and conduct your first YouTube contest. (6) Do it again regularly and refine the process each time.

YouTube for Charities

A s we saw in Chapter 7, YouTube isn't just for businesses. As Richenda Vermuelen demonstrated with her vlogger program at World Vision, you can leverage YouTube to promote your cause. It's not an exaggeration to believe that YouTube can be transformational for charities. From using vloggers to simply using YouTube directly as a marketing tool, the site has enormous potential for helping spread the word about nonprofit efforts.

In this chapter, we'll look at the opportunities that charities have to leverage the powerful possibilities residing in YouTube. We'll also hear from a representative of one of the most prominent media ministries in the United States as we discuss YouTube with the social media direc-tor at the Potter's House, part of T.D. Jakes Ministries in Dallas, Texas.

Four Advantages That Charities Have

Charities have four real advantages over for-profit business when it comes to using YouTube:

1. People expect charities to boldly declare their mission state-ment and reason for existence. The positioning in the market-place can be very clear and compelling. Every charity can have an anchorperson-style video that begins with the statement, "At

_____ we are passionate about solving _____." This type of video can be gripping. It can truly strike a chord with like-minded people and rally people to your cause.

2. Charities generally have a constant stream of content—from still photography that can be turned into videos, to video footage from their events and programs. Unlike for-profit businesses, which are typically hard pressed to come up with this type of content, charities have it in abundance.

3. Charities have a tradition of having a celebrity spokesperson. If yours doesn't, work to find a celebrity who will speak on behalf of your efforts and begin making videos featuring his or her candid support. By default, that person might be your president, executive director, or religious leader. But it can be a celebrity volunteer as well.

4. Charities can use emotional triggers in ways businesses cannot. The deep meaning and closely held convictions that reside deep inside each of us can be identified and included in videos to promote your cause. People are accustomed to this element of charity marketing and welcome it if it's done well. You have permission to make people cry. That's powerful.

YouTube—Your Best Donation of All Time

In a very practical way, by making YouTube a free service, the founders have created a multibillion dollar marketing tool and given it to charities to use for free. For many charities, it could be considered the largest single gift anyone has ever given them. How can charities use YouTube effectively?

Your Basic Opportunities

Let's review the basic opportunities and apply them to the charity context.

Video Hosting Tool

As we discussed in Chapter 1, YouTube is a fantastic video-hosting service. Charities that have a solid stream of video content, such as places of worship, can host the videos on YouTube for free. The videos can be used directly on YouTube for marketing and social media purposes or embedded on your website and used to strengthen your online presentations. This service would have been a massive expense in years gone by. But today it's completely free.

Social Media Platform

As a social media platform, YouTube allows charities to identify and connect with like-minded souls. In upcoming chapters, we'll explore how to do this in lots of very simple yet powerful ways. The conversations and connections that can be made on YouTube are a tremendous boost to nonprofits. Now, instead of connecting with prospects through expensive direct mail, TV, or radio, nonprofits can connect with potential supporters for free. And they can find those supporters from a global (rather than just local) audience.

Search Engine Tool

As the second best search engine online, only behind Google, YouTube is a fantastic tool to spread the news about your charity or social issue. We'll explore this topic in greater depth in a later chapter. How does it work? By effectively using keywords and titles on your videos, you can have content that gets found by searchers looking for your topics of interest. And what is even better is that effective search engine optimization on YouTube positions your content extremely well for displaying in the Google search engine results pages (SERPs). Now, your charity can have a global reach even if it is just a local organization.

Advertising Platform

By leveraging the opportunity to advertise on YouTube, nonprofit marketers have the chance to inexpensively acquire new donors and fans. Marketers can acquire new donors, cultivate existing customers, or upsell existing donors to the next level. In the upcoming chapters, we'll talk about the advertising options available to charities and how they can be used.

Volunteer Engagement Tool

People will work for your charity for free as a volunteer. This one singular advantage over for-profits is a staggering opportunity. Imagine having 1,000 individual fans and supporters create a video for your charity and upload it to their YouTube channels. If each volunteer had just 25 channel subscribers, you'd be reaching an audience of 25,000 people. And if each of the 1,000 videos is watched an average of 100 times, you'd have your story presented to 100,000 people. Those videos will be online for years to come. They will serve as a long-term promotional tool.

In Figure 15.1, you can see our video featuring Esther's Needs Care Center in Lusaka, Zambia—a program we visited in 2009. The video was part of our Liberty Jane Gives Back campaign, a corporate initiative to raise awareness for the plight of orphans and widows.

Figure 15.1 Our video of Esther's Needs Care Center helped raise funds for seamstresses.

For this fun charity campaign, we designated the proceeds of our online auctions to provide sewing and tailoring training and supplies to widows within the Zambian community. We also had the joy of watching as some of our customers became donors to the ministry.

POWER TIP

Learn to effectively use keywords in your video titles, tags, and descriptions so that your videos are highly ranked by YouTube as well as Google in SERPs.

Close Up with the Potter's House—T.D. Jakes Ministries

If you're not familiar with the Potter's House, let me tell you a bit about it. T.D. Jakes is the founder and senior pastor of this 30,000-member megachurch in Dallas, and T.D. Jakes Ministries includes more than 50 separate outreach groups. Jakes has written more than 30 books, many of them featured on the *New York Times* bestsellers list. His organization was honored in 2005 for setting an all-time attendance record at the Georgia Dome for its annual conference. In 2001, *Time* magazine featured Jakes on its cover with the headline, "Is This Man the Next Billy Graham?"

The Potter's House has a YouTube channel (see Figure 15.2) with over 21,000 channel subscribers and 2.3 million video views. Jason Caston is the social media director at the Potter's House. We asked him about the church's YouTube efforts and how the ministry uses the site (you can find it at http://www.youtube.com/thepotterstube) to promote its work.

Figure 15.2 The Potter's House YouTube channel art

■ Q. When and how did you first envision using YouTube for the ministry?

A. We started using YouTube around 2006; we believed that YouTube was the premiere destination for online video so we wanted to make sure we had a presence there. We wanted to make sure that the growing audience that was using YouTube as an online video destination had a way to connect, watch, and interact with the ministry without leaving their favorite video network, YouTube.com.

■ Q. What specific steps have you taken to boost your YouTube results?

A. We have developed a very consistent strategy that consists of awareness, content, and organization. We raise awareness of our YouTube channel by putting it on our offline and on-line marketing materials such as websites, e-mail newsletters, and other ministry marketing materials. We put out at least two to three videos per week since the ministry is always generating video content. Additionally, we organize that content into playlists to make it easy for people to watch exactly what they want to see and not search through our entire video library. With a consistent flow of video content in an organized playlist channel, our online audience continues to share and recommend our videos, and that's how we continue to grow.

■ Q. What were some of your early challenges or struggles?

A. Initially, we chose the wrong name for the YouTube channel. We called it "thepotterstube," which is a good name but not consistent with our other social media properties. We also had issues with our videos having worship music in them and thus generating copyright warnings.

■ Q. How did you overcome them?

A. By the time we researched how to change our YouTube channel user name, we realized two things: (1) it wasn't possible to change user names, and (2) our channel had grown so much in popularity that we didn't want to create a new one. Therefore, we let the channel stay as is, and people seem to actually like the different name. Also, when it comes to copyright issues, we make sure we acknowledge them when the warnings arise so that we do not run afoul of the copyright three-strikes rule that could get our YouTube channel shut down.

■ **Q. What "aha" moments have you experienced where you realized you could do something differently/better to boost your YouTube results?**

A. Our first aha moment was when we learned that people want consistent content. They want to see a channel that updates often and continues to keep the videos coming. Our next aha moment was when we put our videos into playlists, we saw our views increase rapidly because people were able to get to the videos they wanted to watch much more easily. Our last aha moment was when we started to consistently use YouTube tags, and we started to see our views rise because people were finding our videos much more often.

■ **Q. What results or successes have you achieved because of YouTube?**

A. With the popularity and success of our YouTube channel, we have been able to utilize YouTube as a marketing channel and ministry opportunity. When we need to distribute content and get videos out to the public, we can use YouTube as a great distribution network. Also, when it comes to ministry and reaching people where they are, YouTube is a great network. When our pastor wants to minister to thousands online, he can make a YouTube video and people can be reached right through our channel.

■ **Q. If you were sitting down with someone just getting started with YouTube, what advice would you give?**

A. First, I would say to develop a video content strategy. Determine how much video content you can gather and/or create for your YouTube channel. Then determine how often you will put videos out, at least putting out one per week. Next, I would suggest getting a graphic designer to design a nice banner for your channel. Make your channel look visibly appealing and professional. Finally, I would suggest that you start advertising your YouTube channel on all your marketing materials (website, Facebook, Twitter, flyers, etc.) so that people see that you have a YouTube presence.

▪ Q. What common mistakes do you see business owners making on YouTube?

A. The number one mistake is not enough content. Many businesses start out great, but then they taper off and eventually neglect the channel. Therefore, the people who subscribed and want videos from your business eventually forget about your organization. The number two mistake businesses make is putting out a lot of unprofessional videos and/or a channel that looks unprofessional. Your YouTube channel is a representation of your business, and the channel and content should be professional. You don't have to put out professional videos *every* time, but at least take some time to put out a good amount of professional content, because you are running a professional business.

▪ Q. What's your success story with YouTube? How has it changed your life and/or business for the better?

A. YouTube is the second largest search engine in the world, so we knew that if we put our content there, people would want to consume it. Our large YouTube following has taken our ministry to another level online, because each video we upload becomes a ministry opportunity for our church as well as the people who share it. We enjoy seeing thousands of people watch and share our videos, and we enjoy bringing our content to the video network that people love.

■ **Q. What are the biggest mistakes you've made using YouTube that we can help folks avoid?**

A. First and foremost is to name your channel accordingly—make sure you choose a user name that is consistent with your other social media channels. If your company is named Acme and your website is Acme.com, then try to get a YouTube channel named youtube.com/acme. Next, stay consistent with your video content. We currently send out consistent video content, but in the beginning we weren't, and people neglected our channel because they didn't trust that we would give them the content they wanted, even though we had it. Finally, YouTube is a major video channel, a major search engine that has billions of views, but it doesn't have what your organization is offering, so make sure you continue to showcase your organization to the best of your ability.

■ **Q. What are some of the most important techniques or tools you've discovered to help you grow your business with YouTube?**

A. Content, tags, and playlists are major techniques we use to grow our business on YouTube. We continue to distribute content consistently; we make sure we fill out all the tag, title, and description information so that our videos are easily searchable. We also make sure our playlists are utilized for specific topics or events that our users want to watch on our channel.

■ **Q. Can you distill your YouTube advice down into several key tips for readers?**

A. First, develop a video content strategy; then create and/or gather videos for your channel and put them out consistently, at least once a week. Second, make your YouTube channel look professional, have a designer create a cover banner for your channel, and make sure most (not necessarily all) of your videos have a professional feel to them.

Third, utilize playlists and tags. Create playlists that will keep your video content organized and easily accessible on your channel. Also, when you upload your videos, fill out the tags, description, and title information thoroughly because that makes your videos much easier to find by online users. Fourth, communicate with your users via your videos. If online users take time to leave a comment, then address it. If it's positive, then thank them; if they ask a question, then answer; and if it's negative, determine whether you want to respond, delete it, and/or ban them.

And Action!

(1) Consider the ways your charity can use YouTube. (2) Brainstorm ways that you can mobilize volunteers to spread the word about your work. (3) Determine how you can use any existing stream of video content on YouTube. (4) Organize your videos into playlists to ensure they are easy to browse on your channel. (5) Communicate with your users via your videos and comments.

Part 5

GENERATING REVENUE ON YOUTUBE

YouTube

Driving Traffic

ecently, I was asked to fly to Chicago to speak about Pinterest at
the Internet Retailer Conference. It's a massive annual gath-
ering of the top Internet retailers, as well as vendors and retail
e-commerce experts. If you've ever been to the McCormick Center in
Chicago, you know it's a massive place—and this event filled it. My job
was to discuss the latest changes in the Pinterest platform. The room
we were in was just a secondary venue, but it still sat probably 2,000
people. As I always do, I had prepared to start with a brief overview of
our business. My slide show included the graphic shown in Figure 16.1,
which I use in all my presentations to explain our various social media
results and a snapshot of one month's web traffic results.

As you can tell from the figure, we haven't achieved breakout success on any platform. We have a modest amount of website traffic and
a reasonable number of subscribers and followers on the social media
platforms we choose to participate in. You'll notice that we don't use
Twitter, nor do we have any plan to; it's simply never been the platform
that we thought we'd want to participate in—too much hyperactivity. But
overall, we've got a crowd on each platform, the smallest of which is on
Instagram, our newest social media channel.

The speaker just before me was the CEO of a very familiar online
website; I'd imagine you've heard of it. He stood and announced that
his company's website gets 18 million unique visitors per month. Wow!
Talk about being intimidating. I felt embarrassed that I had to even get

up and present after hearing those numbers. What could I possible know? Our tiny little e-commerce site only has 50,000 unique visitors per month (on a really good month). I whipped out my iPhone calculator and did the math: his company's site traffic is 360 times bigger than ours. According to Alexa.com's traffic rankings, the website is one of the top 400 in the United States.

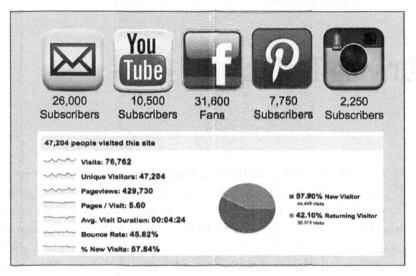

Figure 16.1 The Liberty Jane Clothing social media stats and one month's web analytics for our e-commerce site, http://www.libertyjanepatterns.com

So I'm sitting there embarrassed to go up and present and am feeling a bit unsure of myself, looking around at the 2,000 people and getting generally freaked out. Then the thought occurred to me, "I wonder how many Pinterest followers his company has?" So I looked at the social media stats. Can you guess what I found?

The number of Pinterest followers amounted to 1,340. Ours at Liberty Jane Clothing is 7,750. Hey, I started to feel better. We're a tiny little company, but our Pinterest work was much larger. His company had more than five times the number of Facebook fans than we had, which in the scheme of things isn't that impressive. His company's Instagram profile was smaller than ours. The amount of subscribers to his company's YouTube channel was a bit larger, but not much larger: 16,000 subscribers compared with our 10,500. So in two of the four social media channels I compared, we had a larger presence. I started to feel better.

Sitting there that day, the realization hit me. Good online marketing in today's context is largely about cross-promotion of your online properties, and the new secret ninja skill that no one is talking about is how to drive traffic from one platform to another. Just because you can spend a lot of money buying massive traffic to your website or advertising to get huge numbers of fans on Facebook, that doesn't mean your other social sites are going to scale up without deliberate strategies and tactics. In Chapter 12, we discussed ways to get people moving from one social network to another. In this chapter, we'll talk about getting people both to move from your website to social media and to move from your social media sites to your other online properties.

The Facebook-Only Problem

Another brief example: I am familiar with a local corporation that has annual revenues of several billion dollars. Last I heard, it had a Facebook advertising budget of $2,000 a day. As you'd expect, the company's Facebook fan page is massive—over a million fans. But if you look at its YouTube channel, Pinterest profile, Twitter account, or Instagram profile, you'll see very small results with no real engagement strategy. I'd guess you can find examples of this same phenomenon online.

What have these social media managers done? They've spent millions, I'd guess, investing in the Facebook platform without a plan for how to integrate that effort more broadly. And if you cannot drive traffic from Facebook to YouTube, how in the world will you drive it to your online shopping cart? The answer is that you won't.

POWER TIP

To maximize your ROI from any online advertising efforts, get good at driving traffic from one online location to another. Advertise on Facebook; then get those new fans onto your YouTube channel. In that way, you'll double your opportunity to engage with prospective new customers. The stronger your online bond with prospects, the more likely they are to buy from you.

Needless to say, social media teams that have gone down the Facebook path probably didn't have a good day earlier this year when *Time* magazine announced, "Facebook has lost its cool," citing a Pew Research report. The report says that teens are migrating to newer social media sites because their parents are on Facebook, and they want to "be social" without their parents seeing what they're doing. Will the teens leaving spell the end for Facebook? I don't think Facebook is going to become the next Myspace and watch its subscribers leave in droves. I think it's more likely it's going to become the new yellow pages and white pages, all rolled up into one. But there is a chance it could fall out of favor with the masses. Stranger things have happened. That's a risk you don't want to be exposed to.

The truth is, you can simply buy fans on Facebook as your social media strategy and probably get away with it in a large company. Your Facebook fan page grows to a massive number, and you tell your bosses that Facebook is the platform that really "resonates" with your audience. You downplay the other social media networks and talk about why they're a bad idea for your brand.

Heaven forbid anyone ever ask why you have only 350 subscribers on YouTube, why you have only 600 Instagram followers, or why Facebook seems to be the only thing you've got figured out. You haven't really figured out social media at all. You've simply figured out how to spend company money to buy fans.

The Three Mindsets

As I've mentioned, I have two very different contexts in my marketing work. My day job involves managing a fairly typical marketing team at a university. My evenings and weekends are filled with bootstrapping pandemonium in support of our small, family-owned e-commerce business. So I get to encounter a lot of personality types and perspectives, all within the realm of marketing. I work with some as employees, some as contractors, and still more as vendors. My conclusion is that there are two good ends of the spectrum when it comes to social media managers and the mindsets they bring to their jobs. Then there is a third place that deserves a mention.

The Art Director Mindset

Artistic-minded social media marketers usually have a background in the creative arts—maybe videography, photography, graphic art, or copywriting. They are focused on ensuring that the aesthetic qualities of the social media efforts are top-notch. Beautiful images, pithy quotes, on-message comments. These marketers are creating art on the social media platforms they manage.

If you ask them whether they would prefer to manage five social media platforms and learn to produce content for each one or would rather manage just one platform, they'll usually choose to manage just one. And they'll do it incredibly well.

These social media managers aren't bad at social media. In fact, they are frequently great at social engagement on the channels they manage. Their top priority is high-quality media as a way to attract a social following. But as you might guess, they are less comfortable with the calls to action, the "asks," and the selling. They are also slower to produce content than is frequently needed.

The Direct Response Mindset

The second type of social media manager comes from a direct response marketing background. Maybe the person has managed a direct mail program, maybe a telemarketing team, sales team, or e-mail marketing program. Managers with the direct response mindset are generally not focused on the art or the standards of quality that distinguish the artistic mindset. They are focused on the numbers and on driving results.

These social media managers aren't bad at what they do. They are focused on growth and driving revenue results. They can, however, more frequently do things that are lower quality, off message, and oriented to the short term in their haste to get things done. When they're not careful, they run the risk of damaging the quality of the brand with short-term thinking.

The upside to the direct marketer mindset is that these managers get energized by making an ask, giving a pitch, and closing the sale. When it comes to the direct response aspects of social media, these managers shine. They are very focused on generating revenue results through the various social media properties. You've gotta love that.

The Clueless Mindset

Sadly, as with any other corporate role, there are people who get placed into social media who don't have either the art director mindset or the direct marketer mindset—they simply bounce from random thing to random thing without a clear view toward much of anything. They are the clueless among us.

The most successful social media managers are capable of operating with both productive mindsets. They get the artistic, but they also get the direct response. They weave beauty and art and quality into the social platforms for the purpose of driving results. This is the type of social media manager we should all aspire to become. When we can do that, we can drive traffic from one online context to the next in a professional and high-quality way. Let's look at the specific places we should be driving traffic and then focus on strategies for making that happen.

Destinations for Your Social Media Traffic

We covered the topic of driving traffic from one social media platform to another in Chapter 12 as we explored the idea of your social media sites being like a big online theme park. Now, let's look at best practices for getting YouTube traffic funneled into your sales cycle. There are lots of terrific destinations for your traffic including:

- **Your e-mail list.** E-mail marketing is one of the original (and still one of the best) forms of online marketing. Getting people from YouTube onto your e-mail list can happen in lots of different ways and should be a top goal.

- **Your product page.** Your e-commerce site's product pages are the most vital part of selling online, and getting traffic from YouTube to those pages has got to be a top priority.

- **Your launch list.** A unique e-mail list that will serve you incredibly well is referred to as a "launch list." It's the list of people who have signed up to hear more about your new product or service.

- **Your preorder list.** The next step on the launch sales cycle is to ask people to preorder. Driving them to a preorder launch list is a great use of YouTube.

- **Your auction.** Although it won't apply to every business, if you run special auctions in support of your business, then driving traffic to your auctions via YouTube is helpful.

- **Your event RSVP.** Having people go from YouTube to an RSVP list for your upcoming event is easy to accomplish.

Nine Methods for Generating YouTube Traffic

We covered the topic of driving traffic to various worthwhile locations in the last section. Now let's look at exactly how to do it.

The Scripted Pitch

The easiest and most powerful way to drive traffic from YouTube to your desired location is to simply ask people on your video, "Hey, I'd love to have you visit my eBay auction," etc. The pitch doesn't have to be coercive or forced. Simply ask people to do you a favor, tell them what you've got for them, and outline some of the benefits.

The On-Video Call to Action

The Call-to-Action overlay is a YouTube feature that allows video owners to advertise on their own videos. Instead of having "Tide Ultra Vivid White Detergent" ads pop up on your video, you can have "Visit My Website Now for Your Free Gift" ads pop up on your website. This feature is an incredibly powerful way to drive traffic to your desired locations.

The On-Video Text Box

You can place a text box on your video with a call to action. Technically, this is called an "annotation," and we discussed it in chapter 11. While you can't make a clickable link to an off-YouTube destination, you can simple ask people to "Visit http://www.yourwebsite.com for more information" or to take some other action. If you want, you can add a clickable link to another video, which in some cases is a great solution. For example, if you're doing a product-launch series and the first video explains the major benefits of and reason for the product, then in the subsequent videos you can have an on-video text box at the end that says, "Watch Video One to Learn Why We Created This Product."

The Channel Links

Your channel home page has a series of links that can be used to drive traffic. It's an important way to get traffic off YouTube and onto your websites. If you look at the Google Analytics for Liberty Jane Patterns, you'll notice that the top source of traffic from our YouTube efforts comes from the link on our channel. It's the first place people look when they want to learn more about your company.

The Channel About Tab

The About tab on your channel is where people come to learn more about you. You can use that space to provide a powerful call to action. Create a standing offer for YouTube viewers and mention it there, or simply tell people about your latest product or service launch, sale, or promotion.

The Channel Comments

Your Channel Comments tab is a running list of the interactions you're having with people on your channel. This is a great place to make a call to action and explain the details of a new product or service. You can mention a URL, but you cannot make it clickable.

The Bulletin

There is a little-known function in YouTube that has powerful benefits. The bulletin allows you to place a comment on every one of your subscribers' feeds. You can include a link to one of your videos or even a link to other YouTube videos. Unfortunately, you can't place a clickable link to take people off YouTube, but with some creative writing skills, the bulletin can provide a lot of exposure for your new project.

The Video Description

Your video description box is the most important place to include a URL if you want to drive traffic off YouTube. This text box allows URLs to be clickable links, so you'll want to have the URL be the first thing in the text box. If it's included later in the message, it will likely be excluded from sight when people watch your video in some scenarios. So having it be the first thing in the text box is important. Additionally, you'll want to ensure that the URL you provide is the most relevant destination possible. It can be a deep link to a specific page on your website, rather than simply pointing people to your primary URL. In that way, you can direct people straight to the information you're discussing in the video.

The Video Comments

There are two locations for comments on YouTube: on your channel and on each specific video. So under each video, be sure to give a call to action. While you can't include a clickable link here, you can ask people to visit specific online locations.

The Options Never End

These are just the obvious ways to get traffic from YouTube. Once you begin using the site, you'll discover even more ways. For example, you can begin partnering with other YouTube channel owners in related industries and work together to promote one another. If you find just one such partner, then you've effectively doubled all the options listed here. Imagine having 10 such partners, or 20. Make it your goal to find new ways to advertise your business on YouTube. In the next few chapters, we'll discuss the YouTube advertising program that actually lets you spend money to drive traffic. Adding that functionality to the free options mentioned in this chapter will give you a powerful set of tools to accomplish your traffic goals.

And Action!

(1) Make it your goal to learn how to drive traffic from YouTube to your other social sites and sales funnel destinations. (2) Ensure you don't end up with a Facebook-only problem or with all your traffic at any one location. Double your ROI on new prospects by getting them onto multiple social sites. (3) Identify all the possible methods of driving traffic to your website and start to leverage them. (4) Monitor your results and make goals related to the amount of traffic you can get from YouTube.

Chapter
17

Driving Results via Analytics

I f your YouTube efforts don't drive clear and compelling business results, then you're wasting your time. Sure, there's a place for generally
building your brand and creating a reputation, but most people would
agree that one of the following actions is a top priority:

- Driving traffic to your website

- Assisting in the sales process

- Working to collect e-mail addresses

- Generating advertising revenue

Whatever your specific business goal, you can improve your efforts
over time as you learn what works and what doesn't. YouTube has a wide
variety of analytical tools built right into the site to help you understand
how your marketing efforts are going. Additionally, Google has its own
website analytics product, Google Analytics, that you can use to see how
the website traffic you receive from YouTube is performing. And as if
that is not enough, there are third-party analytics tools that can assist
you in learning more about how things are going. In this chapter, we'll
walk through how to dig into these analytical tools to maximize your
results.

Don't worry; if you're not an analytical person by nature, later in the chapter you'll find 18 lessons you can take away with you from these analytical tools. These insights are designed to help prompt your thinking about how best to use the analytics data.

YouTube Analytics

YouTube Analytics is an analytics package that you can use to evaluate the success of your efforts. The functionality allows you to see your results at both the channel level and the individual video level. To view these features, simply click on the Video Manager option in your user account area (see Figure 17.1). Then, from the Video Manager option, click on the Analytics option on the left-hand side (see Figure 17.2).

Figure 17.1 The Video Manager is accessed from your YouTube settings.

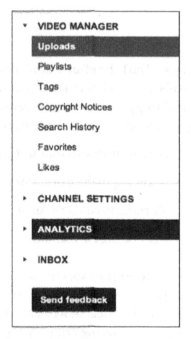

Figure 17.2 The Analytics option is found under the Video Manager area.

Let's review the types of information you can look at through YouTube Analytics.

■ **Overview.** From the Overview tab, you can view a summary of your performance and engagement metrics. This is intended to be a quick snapshot of your accounts performance.

■ **Earnings reports.** The earnings reports provide a summary of your revenue from monetization efforts.

■ **Estimated earnings report.** The estimated earnings report displays the total estimated earnings for the time period chosen. The convenient line chart also allows you to see the daily results.

■ **Ad performance report.** The ad performance report shows the playback-based CPM, the gross earnings, and the amount of estimated monetized playbacks. CPM stands for cost per thousand, and the playback-based CPM report estimates your gross revenue per thousand playbacks on which an ad was shown.

■ **Views reports.** The views reports are intended to provide detailed information about your viewership and your viewers' behavior. The Views Reports tab includes:

   ■ **Views.** The views report shows you total video views for the given date range. This report also shows you the estimated minutes watched.

   ■ **Demographics.** The demographics report identifies the percentage of male versus female viewers by country. This report also shows you your top locations (countries) and the age ranges of your viewers. At Liberty Jane Clothing, our viewers are 85 percent female, and the largest age group is 35 to 44.

   ■ **Playback locations.** The playback locations report shows you where people are watching your videos, such as on mobile devices, the YouTube watch page, embedded videos on your website, the YouTube channel page, or other YouTube pages. At Liberty Jane Clothing, 65 percent of our views come from mobile devices. This report also shows you the average minutes watched by location and the average view duration.

   ■ **Traffic sources.** The traffic sources report lets you know the origin of the viewers. Sources can include mobile apps, direct traffic, YouTube searches, home feeds and subscriptions, external websites, Google searches, and more.

- **Devices (beta).** The devices report gives you information about the types of devices your viewers are using. Options include computers, tablets, mobile phones, TV, unknown, and game consoles.

- **Audience retention.** The audience retention report shows you the average view duration at the channel level and also the average view duration for each video you have uploaded. Additionally, this report allows you to overlay another metric for purposes of comparison. For example, you can compare your average view duration with your total estimated earnings to gain insight into how your view duration affects your earnings.

- **Engagement reports.** The engagement reports are designed to provide information about your subscribers and their involvement with your videos and channel. The engagement reports include:

- **Subscribers.** The subscribers report provides the total number of subscribers gained or lost for the time duration being viewed. You can also find the actual number of subscribers both gained and lost. In addition, you can see which videos have resulted in subscribers being gained or lost.

- **Likes and dislikes.** The likes and dislikes report provides a summary of the total number of likes and dislikes at both the channel level and individual video level. The information is also sorted by video, country, and date.

- **Favorites.** The favorites report presents the total number of favorites by country as well as date range. You can also see the number of favorites added or removed by video.

- **Comments.** The comments report shows the total number of comments for the channel as well as for individual videos for the date range selected. This report also includes the total engagement results by video, which is a sum of the total number of likes, dislikes, favorites added and removed, shares, comments, subscribes, and unsubscribes.

- **Sharing.** The sharing report indicates the total number of times sharing has occurred for a given date range or according to geographic location. It also allows you to see the sharing service that was used.

- **Call to action.** The call-to-action report provides the total number of call-to-action impressions and clicks. It also calculates the click-through rate for you.

- **Annotations (beta).** The annotations report supplies data about how your video annotations are performing. It includes click-through rates as well as close rates, which are the percentage of annotation impressions that were closed by the viewer.

Google Analytics

Google Analytics provides information for webmasters about the traffic coming to the site. There is a section related to social traffic, which documents the results of YouTube visitors coming to your website.

Google Analytics can also be configured to capture e-commerce revenue and document the source of the traffic that led to the purchasing behavior. In that way, you can determine if traffic from YouTube outperforms traffic from Facebook or other top sites. To see the social media–related data in Google Analytics, look under the Traffic Sources tab and then follow through to the section labeled "Social." The following reports are just a part of what is available:

- **Overview.** The overview report shows the social networks referring visitors to your website. The networks are ordered from largest referrer to smallest. You can see visits, total page views from each social network, average visit duration, and average number of pages per visit.

- **Network referrals.** The network referrals report identifies the individual links within each social network that sent traffic to your site. You can drill down to see the specific URL on the social network that is sending traffic to your website. When looking at the results from YouTube, you can see the traffic that resulted from each video.

- **Visitor flow.** The visitor flow report shows you the path that visitors take when coming from social media sites, including YouTube. You see the page they land on as well as any subsequent pages visited.

Third-Party Analytics—Social Blade

There are interesting third-party websites that provide additional insight into your YouTube work. One valuable tool that is worth learning to use is Social Blade (http://www.socialblade.com). What is incredibly interesting about Social Blade is that the site allows you to see detailed YouTube results for any channel. In other words, it gives you the tools to spy on your competitors and see what is working for them. On the site, you'll get free access to the following reports:

> **POWER TIP**
>
> Wondering how your competitors are doing on YouTube? Use Social Blade to see their results. Learn from their successes and discover the types of videos that are capturing people's interest.

- **Subscriber goal report.** The subscriber goal report calculates your subscriber growth rate and calculates how many days it will take until you reach the next major subscriber milestone. Regardless of the size of your subscriber list, this report forecasts your growth toward your next major milestone.

- **View goal report.** The view goal report forecasts the number of days it will take to reach your next major channel view milestone, whether it's 10,000 views or 100 million.

- **Daily stats report.** The daily stats report allows you to see the changes in your number of subscribers over the prior 24-hour period. You can see the number of subscribers who have joined your list hour by hour.

- **Monthly stats report.** The monthly stats report allows you to see subscribers, video views, channel views, contacts, and estimated earnings. The data are displayed on a day-by-day basis and also show any changes from the prior day.

- **Other channels box report.** The other channels box report shows you which YouTube channels are including a link to your YouTube channel. In other words, this tells you which channels on YouTube are referring people to your channel.

- **Similar ranked channels report.** The similar ranked channels report shows you channels that are of a similar size to yours. This may be less appealing for some businesses than others, since it's not specific to a niche or industry. But it can still shed some interesting light on your efforts.

- **Videos report.** The videos report itemizes the last 25 videos that have been updated and the views associated with them. This is an incredibly handy feature, especially when you are looking at your competitors' results. Seeing how their last 25 videos have performed helps you understand what the prospects in your niche or industry are engaging with. The video report displays the following information for the last 25 videos:

  - Published date

  - Video length in minutes and seconds

  - View count

  - Average rating

  - Number of ratings

  - Number of favorites

  - Number of comments

  - Estimated video earnings—this statistic is an estimated range of earnings based on the AdWords CPM views. The data are presented as a range because not all ads pay the same amount. However, the information is helpful in getting a general sense of the advertising revenue results.

18 Insights to Discover from Your Analytics

Let's look at the insights you can gain from your analytics and which analytics tool you can discover the information on, including YouTube Analytics (YTA), Social Blade (SB), and Google Analytics (GA).

1. Which videos are the most viewed? Although you need to consider the age of the video and account for older videos having more views than newer videos, you can still see popular videos in this way. The real question is which type of video you should continue to do more of. (YTA)

2. Which of your competitors' videos are the most popular? You can see this information by looking at their accounts on Social Blade. By determining which videos they've published that are popular, you can get ideas about new videos to produce. (SB)

3. Which videos are the most liked, favorited, and commented on? You should be able to see why, but the findings might surprise you. Asking the question "why?" should reveal interesting answers. (YTA)

4. Which video is the most disliked? What have you done to generate the most thumbs-down responses, and what can you learn from it? Was the video quality bad, or did you share something that your audience disagrees with? (YTA)

5. Which video prompted the most people to subscribe? This information is helpful because it enables you to see if certain calls to action work better than others. It also sheds light on the type of video that people are most interested in watching. (YTA)

6. Which video prompted the most people to unsubscribe? What lesson can you learn? Try to evaluate if it is the style of video, the quality of the video, the script, or the general topic that people are not interested in. (YTA)

7. What is the rate of growth for your channel? Is your growth rate meeting your expectations? What can you do to accelerate your subscribership growth? (SB)

8. What is your next major milestone in terms of both subscribers and video views? Can you celebrate the milestone or even ask your customers to help you reach it more quickly? (SB)

9. What's the average age of your subscribers? Are you creating videos that appeal to that age group? You might consider adding on-screen guests or video talent that matches that age group. (YTA)

10. What's the percentage of male versus female viewers? Are you engaging with a mostly female or male audience, and does that support your product line and sales strategy? (YTA)

11. What devices are your subscribers using to watch your videos? Are smartphones the most common device? That might suggest your videos should be relatively short and easily viewed on a small screen. (YTA)

12. What are the top three countries that the majority of your subscribers come from? Is there anything you can do to create content that appeals even more to countries number two and three with the hope of boosting their engagement? (YTA)

13. How much money are you making from your videos via YouTube's program? Interested to see what your competitors are making on YouTube? Consider looking up their profiles on Social Blade for a range of revenues based on the potential high and low CPMs that their channels are generating. (SB)

14. How much money are you making from customers who come to your website from YouTube? Are they a profitable group of visitors according to the e-commerce tracking in Google Analytics? How does their purchasing behavior compare with that of traffic from other sources, such as Facebook or Pinterest? (GA)

15. How long do visitors coming to your website from YouTube stay on your site? Are they highly engaged and spending a lot of time on your website, or do they leave quickly? (GA)

16. How long do people watch your videos? Are people watching your videos to the end? Or do they only watch 30 or 40 percent? If the duration is too long, you might consider making your videos briefer. (YTA)

17. How are your calls to action working? Are people clicking on your Call-to-Action overlays at a good percentage? If not, can you make your call-to-action wording more compelling? (YTA)

18. How are your video annotations working? Are people clicking through from one video to the next? If not, do your annotations appear too late in your video? Should you move them closer to the middle or front so that people see them before they get bored and leave? (YTA)

And Action!

(1) Get to know the YouTube Analytics tool and the information it provides. (2) Visit http://www.socialblade.com and see if the insights and lessons it can provide are of value to your business. (3) Look at your Google Analytics for insights into how to optimize your efforts. (4) Begin to identify your mysterious challenges and see if you can find a way to use analytics to add clarity and insight.

Advertising on YouTube

I grew up in Northern California with a grandpa who liked to fish. We'd fish for catfish in the canals and bypasses of the Sacramento River and nearby rice fields. Then we'd drive up to the Sierra Nevadas to fish for trout. It was one of the highlights of my childhood. He wasn't much for explaining things, but he was a great angler. I'd pick up his tricks mostly by watching.

One trick I learned from him was that you want to go where the fish are and the fishermen aren't. If we drove up and there were too many cars parked on the side of the road, too many guys standing on the banks, and too many lines in the water, he'd keep driving or we'd start walking until we didn't see people. Fishing where there are too many people is a drag. So you have to venture into the wilderness a bit. These days, everybody advertises on Facebook and Google AdWords. YouTube, by comparison, feels like the wilderness to me.

Why is YouTube a less common advertising destination? It goes back to the issues we looked at in Chapter 3—corporations are terrible at YouTube. And if they aren't using YouTube effectively for social media marketing, chances are they won't try to use it for advertising purposes. Why not? I can think of three reasons.

1. They are afraid of being embarrassed. They don't want to have an ad on YouTube, and then have people visit their channel and see that they only have 264 subscribers.

2. YouTube is so far off their radar that they don't even consider the idea of advertising on it, because they don't use it for video hosting or social media work.

3. They assume that in order to advertise on YouTube, they have to create an expensive video.

In this chapter, we'll walk through the advertising options on YouTube and discuss the various methods you can use. This chapter is intended to be an introduction to the topic. If you want to "go deep," then there are lots of online resources available to you. I've collected a nice batch you can access at http://www.pinterest.com/jasonmiles/ instagram-power-book. Before we look at the advertising options, let's discuss the two factors to evaluate the success of any advertising campaign.

The Two Factors of a Good Advertising Campaign

A good advertising campaign will demonstrate success in two ways. As an advertiser, you'll want to constantly evaluate these two issues. They are really where the rubber meets the road. They are also the aspects of an advertising program that make it truly scalable, meaning you can spend more and more money because you know you're getting a good return on your investment. What are the factors?

1. The Cost of the Traffic

Traffic can cost you nothing, or it can cost you a lot. The most common method for determining the cost of advertising on most online platforms is referred to as CPC (cost per click). You've probably heard that term before. So you can compare the CPC of Facebook ads versus Google AdWords ads versus YouTube ads. One prominent feature of the YouTube advertising program is the relatively low cost that you can achieve. You can get clicks for pennies; and in a few pages, I'll show you how to get them for free. But cost isn't the only issue you need to consider.

2. The Performance of the Traffic

The people who visit your commerce site (aka your traffic) are prospects. Will they buy? They will be either good prospects or bad prospects, depending on whether they are willing to buy or not. Over time you can evaluate the quality of your traffic by looking at the Google Analytics and evaluating the e-commerce results. Sadly, you can get lots of junk traffic, and it is a waste of your time. "Junk" traffic is traffic that doesn't convert from prospect to customer. Junk traffic consists of visitors who don't buy. So you'll have to determine if the traffic you get from YouTube is good traffic for your business. That will be different for every advertiser, which is why no one can say, across the board, that YouTube traffic is great. It will be great for some companies and poor for others.

Great success is found when your traffic outperforms the cost of acquiring it—in other words, when you can say, "We make more from these visitors than we spend getting them to show up." That's the holy grail, because when you achieve it, you can scale your efforts up dramatically. If you're making money, why not double your advertising budget? So again, cost isn't everything. If your traffic costs you $10 per click, but you make $10.50 for each click, then you don't really care about the high cost because you're making money. Conversely, if your traffic costs you two cents per click, but you only earn one cent per click, then you probably don't want to scale that effort up, because you're losing money.

These two variables and the way in which they collide spell success or failure for all online advertisers, whether you're Coca-Cola or a brand-new seller on Etsy. So the most logical thing to do, regardless of the size of your operation, is to continually search for new sources of traffic, try to optimize your conversion results, and evaluate how the traffic performs for you. Google Analytics provides information to help you evaluate these issues, but many marketers supplement Google Analytics with additional tools. One we like a lot for landing pages is http://www.unbounce.com. It has fantastic templates that allow you to set up a sales page very quickly. Then it lets you conduct simple split tests to see which combinations of words and pictures work best to convert visitors into customers.

The Six Places to Advertise on YouTube

Don't be overwhelmed by the options available to you for advertising on YouTube. There are actually only six places to advertise. Let's discuss them.

1. **Advertise *in* your own videos.** If you've followed the advice previously outlined in this book, then your video work will be an effective advertisement for your business. You are therefore advertising *in* your video.

2. **Advertise *on* your own videos.** It might seem counterintuitive, but one of the smartest things you can do is leverage the YouTube advertising system to advertise on your own videos. If you've done a good job making the video and you have a good call to action, then you've already advertised *in* your video. But now you can also advertise *on* your video. Why?

   - When you advertise on your own videos, you boost your opportunity to drive traffic from your videos to your website. It's like putting your videos on steroids by giving the viewers a very clear and simple way to click from the video to your website.

   - When you advertise on your own videos, you ensure that your competition cannot advertise on them. Yes, you can disable monetization options on your videos so people cannot advertise on them; but still, if there is a chance for others to drive traffic off YouTube and onto their e-commerce website, you want to ensure it's not your competitors.

3. **Advertise *in* someone else's videos.** Although it's not common for small businesses to do this, you can coordinate with any video creators who are open to it and arrange to have them weave your brand into their next video. This is a common tactic for the large Fortune 500 brands, but it is available to anyone to use.

4. **Advertise *on* someone else's videos.** As long as the person who has created a video has enabled the monetization option on the video, then you can potentially advertise on it using the YouTube advertising system. This is the most common form of YouTube advertising, as it leverages the talent of other video creators in your niche or industry without having to create a formal contract with them.

5. **Advertise across the YouTube site.** You can run banner ads on YouTube that are 300 pixels by 250 pixels. They appear to the right of the featured video and above the video suggestions list. You can even have the http://www.youtube.com home page all to yourself

for an entire day. These "red-zone" ads run upward of $300,000, according to searchenginewatch.com.

6. **Advertise on the YouTube mobile platform.** A growing percentage of YouTube video views are occurring through mobile devices. By using the YouTube mobile platform, you can design ads that work effectively in that format. Generally, to advertise on the mobile platform, you need to work with a YouTube sales representative. However, if you set up a Call-to-Action overlay, as we'll describe in a moment, you have the option of having those ads displayed on mobile devices. You can connect with the Google team and learn more at http://www.youtube.com/yt/advertise/mobile.html.

Advertising Formats

YouTube has advertising options for businesses of all sizes. Some options are only relevant to large companies, so we won't focus on those. Instead, we'll look at the options available to everyone. There are four basic advertising methods on YouTube. They're powered by Google AdWords for video. Some you can set up yourself directly, and some require that you speak to a YouTube sales representative. Let's review the formats, and then we'll look at another option, the Call-to-Action overlay.

TrueView Ads

The YouTube TrueView campaign options allow you to create ad formats in five unique ways.

1. **TrueView in-search ads.** The in-search ads appear above and to the right of the regular results that appear on the video search results page. These ads operate as other Google AdWords ads do. You create a campaign and add keywords, and your results are based on your competitive bidding.

2. **TrueView in-display ads.** The in-display ads appear alongside videos and even on websites that are on the Google Display Network that are a match for your target audience.

3. **TrueView in-stream ads.** These ads play like a TV-style ad before, after, or during the video they're running on. The ads are run on

YouTube Partner videos. The nice part about these ads is that you only pay if viewers watch for at least 30 seconds or to the end of the video, whichever is less. To understand how to set up an in-stream ad, YouTube requires that you contact a sales representative. You can do that at http://www.youtube.com/advertise_signup.

4. **TrueView in-slate ads.** In-slate ads run on YouTube Partner videos that are 10 minutes or longer. Viewers choose to watch one of three ads or see regular commercial breaks during their video instead.

5. **Pre-roll ads.** Pre-roll ads run before the video begins. They are classic-looking commercials. Generally this is the domain of the larger-brand advertisers. Pre-roll ads enable you to target your audience by specific geographic, demographic, or topic criteria. You can even re-market to people who have previously enjoyed your content on YouTube or on Google Display Network. Pre-roll ads also work on the mobile platform as well as the traditional desktop viewing context.

Rather than try to give you a step-by-step tutorial on how to set up these various advertising campaigns, I'm simply going to recommend that you jump onto YouTube and begin the process, guided by the site's terrific video tutorials (see Figure 18.1). You can get started immediately at:

- http://www.youtube.com/yt/advertise
- http://www.youtube.com/yt/promoteyourself/

Figure 18.1 The YouTube advertising and promotion options make it easy for you to get started.

Call-to-Action Overlay

The Call-to-Action overlay is a very common format that is easy to use (see Figure 18.2). This format is one that you can run on your own videos very easily, and you can do it for next to nothing. Most marketers don't know how to do this, and they waste a huge opportunity to drive traffic from their videos to their websites. Here are the steps involved:

POWER TIP

The Call-to-Action overlay is the YouTube marketer's best-kept secret. Unlock it for all your videos and use it to drive traffic to your websites.

Figure 18.2 The Call-to-Action overlay with the headline "Doll Clothes Designers" was added to this video after the feature was "unlocked."

1. Unlock the Call-to-Action overlay feature. The Call-to-Action overlay is "unlocked" for any one of your videos that has been featured in an in-search advertising campaign, as mentioned above

(see Figure 18.3). So the practical thing to do is to feature each of your videos in an in-search ad campaign. That will enable the Call-to-Action overlay function for all your videos. The amazing part is that even when you end the ad campaign and stop paying for the advertisement, the Call-to-Action overlay will remain on the video after it has been set up. It's as if YouTube is offering it to you as a bonus gift for advertising your video. One important note: if you've set your video to be made available for monetization, then you cannot run your own Call-to-Action overlay on that video. So turn off the monetization for the video you want to promote.

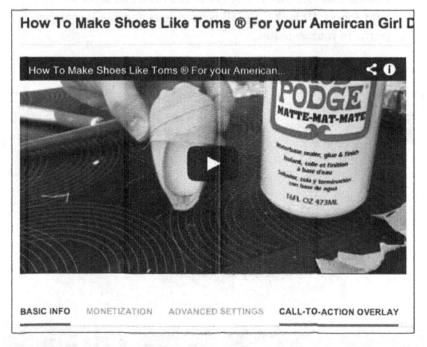

Figure 18.3 The "Call-to-Action overlay" section is revealed in the "Info & Settings" section of the video after you include it in an advertising campaign.

2. Fill in the call-to-action message. You can access the Call-to-Action overlay information under the "Info & Settings" feature of your video. You'll be asked to fill in the following information:

- **Headline.** No more than 25 characters.
- **Description line 1.** No more than 35 characters.

- **Description line 2.** No more than 35 characters.

- **Image URL.** The image must be hosted somewhere. We use Photobucket.

- **Display URL.** This is the URL you want to show on the ad.

- **Destination URL.** This is the URL you want your visitors to arrive at when they click.

- **Enable on mobile.** You'll be given an option to enable your Call-to-Action overlay on mobile.

When the information is entered, you simply hit Save. Your new Call-to-Action overlay will display on your video (see Figure 18.4). If you don't see it, remember to check your monetization settings and ensure they are off for the video you're attempting to run your call-to-action overlay on.

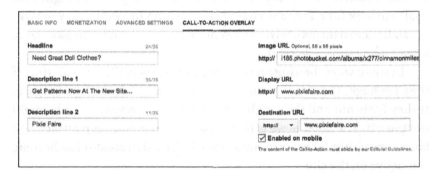

Figure 18.4 The Call-to-Action overlay is not visible until your video has been included in a marketing campaign.

Advertising in Other People's Videos

One of the strongest selling options on YouTube is to have a video maker do a testimonial or recommendation for your product or service. These types of one-off arrangements are more difficult to arrange, but they will position your brand extremely well with that video creator's audience. And if that person has a massive audience, you can get a massive number of impressions. A few of the benefits of arranging one-off advertising agreements include:

- Custom advertising that will be completely unique and creative.

- Advertising that will be inside the video and therefore viewable for as long as the video is on YouTube, which could be many years.

- The power of the video makers' third-party endorsement to their audience. You can leverage the powerful reputation of third parties and the respect the audience has for them.

- The fact that custom advertising is generally worked out for a flat fee; this means the more views that accumulate and the more traffic you get from the video ad, the cheaper the traffic becomes over time.

If you're wondering how best to find and arrange these types of one-off agreements, begin to search for video makers in your niche who are growing a large audience—but one that is not yet too big. If you wait until their audience is very big, then the cost will likely be very high. Your goal is to look for a YouTube channel owner who fits well with your target audience in terms of style and general approach and who has a large and growing subscribership.

In some ways, betting on new video creators is like speculating. If they get huge, then your prior ads with them will feel like a bargain. If they fizzle out and their audience declines, then your gamble might not pay off. The good news is that popular videos can keep attracting a large viewership for years to come, even if the video creator has become less active on the site.

And Action!

(1) Understand how to evaluate the two metrics that every ad campaign depends upon: cost and results. (2) Learn how to use the six places that are available to you for advertising on YouTube. (3) Run a brief in-search ad for each video you make. (4) Unlock the Call-to-Action overlay function for each of your videos. (5) Explore how to arrange one-off advertising agreements with video creators in your niche or industry.

Monetizing Your YouTube Work

The focus of this book has been on how to use YouTube to market your business, with the assumption that you have products or services to sell. Or in the case of nonprofits, that you have programs you need to promote. Fair enough. But it's not the only way to approach YouTube.

People are making real money on YouTube simply by creating content around a specific niche or industry, building a great audience, and then running ads on their videos. On YouTube this advertising-based revenue pursuit is broadly referred to as "monetizing." If you find yourself passionate about the art of making videos and you are knowledgeable about a specific niche or topic, then maybe you can go productless and make money by working with advertisers.

In this chapter we'll look at how you can set up a basic monetization plan using the normal functionality of YouTube. We'll also explore how you can build your own one-off advertising program for maximum profit. Finally, we'll take a behind-the-scenes glimpse at the industry with Dan Weinstein, the CEO of Collective Digital Studio, an agency in Hollywood that works with some of the biggest names on YouTube.

The Three-Party Advertising Strategy

The first broadcast radio show occurred on Christmas Eve 1906. And from even those pioneering days of radio, free broadcast media has had a challenge. The question is, how do you make and broadcast free entertainment content and still make money doing it? How do you pay the bills and turn your effort into a real business. The answer, of course, is advertising. The "three-party" model is one we've all grown up with in both radio and television. So when YouTube started to see expansive opportunities, it didn't take long to realize that the three-party model' would work well on the platform. One person creates the video, an advertiser pays to sponsor it, and the viewers get to enjoy the experience for free, with the requirement that they watch the advertisement. YouTube's Partner Program is the method YouTube uses to coordinate the three-party advertising options. Let's look at how YouTube has set up this monetization process and walk you through it. Then we'll examine additional ways to make money from advertising.

YouTube Partner Program—How to Monetize Your Videos

The easiest way to make money on YouTube is by allowing ads to run on your videos. When you enable one of your videos to accept advertising, YouTube calls you a "partner," and you're now part of its Partner Program. Once you complete the steps involved, then the Google AdWords system places (you hope) relevant ads on your videos. Then you get paid via Google's AdSense program monthly.

Your first question is probably, can you make any real money doing this? The answer is yes! But to make money that will allow you to quit your day job or talk your boss into setting up a new division in your marketing department, you'll need to develop a large viewership. As you might guess, a handful of subscribers and a few thousand video views aren't going to pay the bills.

Monetization Setup Steps

The process for setting up your videos for monetization is a multistep effort. While it's not difficult to be accepted into the Partner Program and to get going, you do need to meet several criteria. In this section

POWER TIP

Google AdSense is a program that allows website owners and YouTube channel owners to display advertisements. The range of compensation is based on several factors, including the competitiveness of the keywords being targeted and the volume of the site traffic.

we'll go through the steps involved. If you get confused or want to jump onto YouTube and walk through its step-by-step guide, then simply visit https://www.youtube.com/yt/partners/.

For the first step to set up the option to monetize your video, you need to visit your account settings and look for the Advertisements options. You'll notice two options, as shown in Figure 19.1.

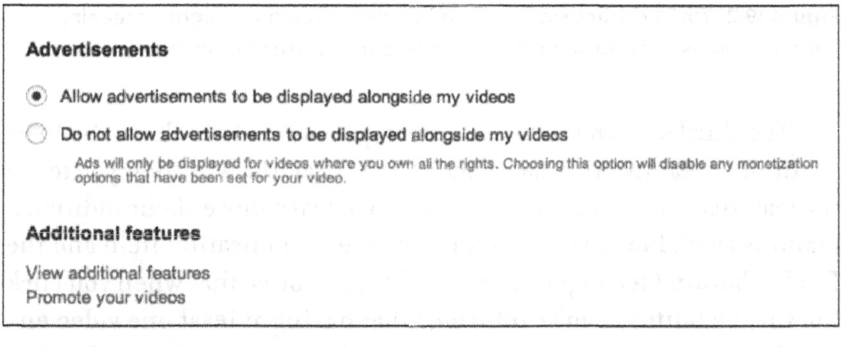

Advertisements

◉ Allow advertisements to be displayed alongside my videos

◯ Do not allow advertisements to be displayed alongside my videos

   Ads will only be displayed for videos where you own all the rights. Choosing this option will disable any monetization options that have been set for your video.

Additional features

View additional features
Promote your videos

Figure 19.1 The Advertising options are located in your YouTube settings. Choosing your option is the first step in setting up monetization.

The second step is to visit your channel settings and ensure your account status indicates that your account is in good standing. You'll want to see a Good Standing indicator next to each of these metrics (see Figure 19.2):

- Community guidelines

- Copyright strikes

- Content ID claims

Features

To enable these features, your account must be in good standing.

Account status

libertyjaneclothing	**Partner**	Verify

Community guidelines	● Good standing
Copyright strikes	● Good standing
Content ID claims	● Good standing

Feature	**Status**	**Description**
Monetization	●	View monetization settings

Figure 19.2 Your account status needs to show three green lights, meaning your account is in good standing, in order to monetize your videos.

The third step in the monetization process is to look for the View Additional Features link (see Figure 19.1). That link will allow you to see the features of your account and help you to learn more about additional features available to you. You'll notice the Monetization item and the Enable button (see Figure 19.3). You'll also notice that when you click the Enable button, you're informed that having at least one video enabled for monetization makes you a YouTube partner. Congratulations! As we mentioned in a previous chapter on uploading your first video, if you'd like to learn more about the Partner Program, visit http://www .youtube.com/yt/creators/.

The fourth step in the monetization process is to read and agree to the YouTube monetization guidelines. There is a wide array of "don'ts" that every video creator needs to understand before placing a video on YouTube. If you want to add the monetizing option to your videos, then you'll need to agree to an additional set of guidelines. It is vital that you read the terms of service (TOS) carefully. Additionally, you must doubly agree to avoid one of the most serious violations in the TOS, which says, "I agree that I will not click on the Google Ads that I'm serving through Google's products and services in order to fraudulently increase

Feature	Status	Description
Monetization	Enable	Become a partner through monetization by displaying ads on your videos. Learn more
Longer videos	Enable	Upload videos longer than 15 minutes. Learn more
External annotations	●	Lets you link annotations to external sites or merch partners. Learn more
Custom thumbnails	●	Lets you use custom thumbnails for your videos. Your account isn't eligible at this time. Learn more
Content ID appeals	●	Lets you appeal rejected Content ID disputes. Learn more
Unlisted and private videos	●	Lets you have unlisted and private videos. Learn more
Live events	●	Lets you create a live streaming event. Your account isn't eligible at this time. Learn more

Figure 19.3 The process of enabling monetization is an option on your account that must be selected.

income." Finally, you must agree to "Not opt-in any content for monetization for which I do not possess sufficient rights." You must assume that these two special agreements represent some of the most problematic aspects of YouTube's monetization program.

The fifth step in the monetization process is to choose the ad formats that you're willing to allow. You're provided with this check box immediately after affirming the guidelines.

The sixth step is to associate your AdSense account with your YouTube channel. Your AdSense account is the way in which you get paid from Google. Once you set up your account, you can receive money from advertising on YouTube or running AdSense ads on your blog or website.

You associate your AdSense account with your YouTube channel by visiting the monetization option in your channel settings. You'll see a drop-down menu that says, "How will I get paid?" The drop-down menu for that question provides the link to associate your account. If you don't have an AdSense account, you'll be directed to create one.

The final step in monetizing your videos is to select Monetize for each of the videos that you want to monetize. You can turn on or turn off the monetization function at the video level. You do that under the "Video Manager" section.

You know you've completed the setup process effectively when you see the status bar completed, as in Figure 19.4.

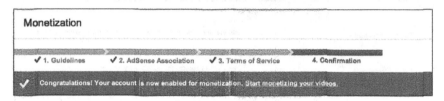

Figure 19.4 Your account status needs to show three green check marks, meaning your account is enabled for monetization.

Making Sponsored Videos

Another way to monetize is to work directly with marketers to place their messages into your videos, as we outlined in Chapter 18. Creating sponsored videos is a very viable way to get bigger paydays. Whereas in Chapter 18 you were the marketer trying to find creators, now you're the creator trying to find a brand to work with. Now you're on the other side of the table, and you've got to work to find ways to get paid to make videos. YouTube has a set of guidelines around sponsored videos. There is a set of dos and don'ts that you need to be familiar with. To see the full guidelines, visit https://support.google.com/youtube/answer/154235.

The principles will feel familiar to you when you're on the video-maker side of the table. You want to do the following:

1. Find a niche and create content that engages an audience around that topic or idea.

2. Create a style that people appreciate. Maybe it's educational, co-medic, or how-to. You want to satisfy people's motivated self-interest or curiosity.

3. Work hard to build an audience and increase video views.

4. Identify potential brands that are a match for your work and reach out to them. You can be passive if you want and wait until they approach you. But if you're anxious to build a revenue stream, then you'll want to be proactive.

Advertising Networks

It's not surprising that if you are a video creator with a passion for making amazing content, you might dislike the process of closing deals with advertisers. Or you might like it, but you don't have the connections to really capitalize on your work. If you're in that situation, you can simply keep using the basic Partner Program and collect money via AdSense. But that will feel limiting in some ways. Or you can consider getting someone to help you work with the advertisers. You can ask a professional to help broker the deals and work with the advertisers. This concept has grown into what is generally referred to as "ad networks," groups of video creators who are represented by an agency. The agency helps coordinate the advertising opportunities.

Close Up with Dan Weinstein at Collective Digital Studio

We had the privilege of connecting with one such agency—Collective Digital Studio (CDS; see Figure 19.5)—and discussing the topic of the agency's work with its CEO, Dan Weinstein. Dan gives us a behind-the-scenes look at this fascinating world of big brands and big YouTube stars.

Figure 19.5 CDS's YouTube channel art

> ■ **Q. Can you tell us about CDS and the role it is playing in the marketplace?**
>
> **A.** CDS is one of the preeminent multichannel digital networks, producing, distributing, and marketing digital content geared to the coveted millennial generation. CDS

boasts some of the top digital content channels across comedy, entertainment, music, and food and a talent lineup that equates to a true "Dream Team" of digital influencers led by Dane Boedigheimer (Annoying Orange), Freddie Wong and Brandon Laatsch (FreddieW), Harley Morenstein (Epic Meal Time), Rhett McLaughlin and Link Neal (Rhett & Link), Hannah Hart (My Drunk Kitchen), and Megan and Liz Mace (Megan & Liz). Headed by this lineup of Internet stars, CDS's content currently garners more than 400 million views per month across its network of more than 300 premium channels that it exclusively distributes and monetizes. The studio's ability to work with its talent on seamless, authentic brand integrations has consistently attracted the attention of Madison Avenue and industry heavyweights ranging from Dodge, Samsung, and Gillette, to Sprint, Dole, 20th Century Fox, and Paramount, who have turned to CDS to develop impactful digital video marketing initiatives. CDS is also the chief architect and producer of the multiplatform successes *Fred: The Movie* (Nickelodeon), *The High Fructose Adventures of the Annoying Orange* (Cartoon Network), and *Video Game High School* (YouTube/Netflix). We are leading the charge in premium entertainment geared toward millennials online.

■ **Q. What value proposition do you offer to YouTube video makers that they cannot get on their own?**

A. This depends on the creator, but we have built an infrastructure to better monetize (through sponsorship and ad sales) content, produce larger-scale projects, finance specific initiatives, help market and build audience, deploy technology for myriad initiatives, and transition from YouTube star/creator to global cross-platform brands. We also coordinate ad sales, production, financing, marketing and audience development, technology, and management.

■ **Q. It seems like most of your channels are young comedy-oriented channels. Is there a similar service for craft, makeup, cooking-type (arts/crafts/beauty) channels?**

A. Yes. We have a burgeoning fashion/beauty/lifestyle vertical (anchored by a relationship with Estèe Lauder) as well as music, kids and family, gaming, etc. All primarily focused on the millennial audience.

■ **Q. Is there a minimum subscribership or number of video views you need to see in order to accept a channel?**

A. No. We pride ourselves on working with talented creators and performers at any stage of their development. Talent can come from anywhere. We have some developing talent as well as some creators that have some of the largest audiences online. It's more about the talent and the opportunity for us rather than the scale.

■ **Q. What other criteria do you look for when considering whether to add a channel?**

A. Are they talented, is their opportunity beyond what they are currently doing, do they fit into a vertical we are currently working with, are they brand friendly, etc.

■ **Q. Are there channels that wouldn't be a good match for your service?**

A. No, we are right for everyone . . . especially those that speak to a demo that we don't talk to very much like moms, etc., but if you are a talented individual and speak to a millennial audience, we could probably help.

■ **Q. How do you ensure a good match between the brand (advertiser) and the channel/video content?**

A. This is always the challenge. It's important to understand that it is just as important to be authentic and genuine with the audience as it is to get across a brands message. When we can integrate a product that fits with the core consumer of our talent/influencer and come up with a creative way to tell a story or enable that content through the brand and be up front with the audience, that's when we have the best success. Trying to trick the audience never works, and both brand and creator need to be on the same page. We have been able to do this very well time and time again.

■ **Q. Is there an "average result" that your channels experience when they join CDS?**

A. The measure for success is different for everyone. For some it is about increasing their audience. For others it is about exploiting that audience in other and more scaled ways; in the case of the Annoying Orange it was creating a global media property through TV and merchandising. We look at every creator as an individual opportunity.

■ **Q. Are there rules of thumb you share with channel owners about what level of revenue they should expect from their work? Like a million video views should result in X dollars?**

A. This is very hard to predict since it really depends on a lot of different variables: composition of audience (United States versus the world), consumption habits (mobile versus web), scale of audience, engagement of audience, do they speak to a broad audience or a specific niche/demo, time of year (Q4 versus Q1), are they brand friendly, etc. It's hard to create a formula or template, as everything is different.

■ **Q. If you were sitting down with brand-new YouTube users and they wanted to really grow their personal or business brand via YouTube, what basic advice would you give them as a starting point?**

A. Content marketing and audience development are as important as simply creating good content. Understanding where your potential audience is and who the members of that audience are so you can serve them . . . stick to a schedule, make things that are shareable and invest a lot of time . . . there are very few overnight successes.

■ **Q. What common mistakes do you see business owners make related to YouTube?**

A. Lack of authenticity and engagement. Understand the platform is a two-way conversation and produce content and engage with it as such. Don't just publish or "post and pray."

■ **Q. What are some of the most important techniques or tools you've discovered that help grow a YouTube business (in terms of channel subscribers, video views, and e-commerce/traffic)?**

A. There is no secret sauce. There is hard work, dedication, making great content that people want to watch and more importantly share. Collaboration with people or entities that have a built-in audience doesn't hurt either.

■ **Q. Can you distill your top YouTube tips down into a few suggestions for people who want to use it for business/revenue results?**

A. Know your audience, know the demo, know the platform, and operate by its rules.

And Action!

(1) If you don't have a product to sell, then consider monetizing through the YouTube Partner Program. (2) Consider creating sponsored videos to work directly with brands in your niche or industry. (3) Evaluate offers from brands outside your niche or industry and consider it a creative challenge to produce something that will be fun for your audience but that will also work for the brand. (4) Be proactive in seeking promoted video opportunities. (5) As your work grows, consider finding an ad network to help represent you.

Conclusion

Conclusion

Four Challenges Every Marketer Faces

Hey, marketer—you gonna do anything about what you've read in this book? Gonna create a YouTube strategy that will work for your business? You willing to do what it takes to break through the barriers that have held you back? I hope so. My goal was to write a book that provided you with the reasons why YouTube matters, the examples necessary to inspire action, and the tactical recommendations to get up and running fast. But maybe you've got another option that is better than YouTube. Maybe you've got another trick up your sleeve.

But if you're still debating what to do next, and if you're still contemplating whether to jump into a YouTube marketing strategy as an aggressive next step, then I'll leave you with these four questions:

1. **Is the solution you're going to implement scalable?** Meaning, can you drive serious traffic to your website from it? There are lots of ways to get small amounts of traffic, but very few will really scale to a massive level. YouTube marketing can scale.

2. **Is the solution to your traffic-generation needs time-tested?** Traffic fads come and go. But to really grow a marketing program, you need a solution that has been around for years and will be around for many more. Video is a medium that is time-tested.

3. **Is the marketing initiative you're proposing inexpensive?** Yeah, you could buy a Super Bowl ad this next year, and that would drive some results. But that's probably not in your budget. You need a solution that is inexpensive and can start working with little or no up-front costs. YouTube marketing is cheap.

4. **Does the method you want to use provide long-lasting results?** Let me ask you—what did that tweet you sent out three years ago do for you today? How about that Facebook post? How about that display ad you ran on the Google Ad Network? You need a marketing plan that enables long-lasting benefits. In other words, your advertising work needs a long "shelf life." YouTube videos drive traffic and results for years.

As we wrap up our time together, let me leave you with a final checklist of the activities and actions needed to really crush it on YouTube:

1. Decide on the specific business benefits that YouTube can add to your marketing efforts.

2. Identify any corporate challenges to setting up your new YouTube effort and commit to addressing them.

3. Dwell on the three uses for a YouTube video channel: video hosting, social networking, and advertising.

4. Review the most common mistakes and determine to avoid them.

5. Remember that there are only two reasons people will watch a video—motivated self-interest and curiosity.

6. Choose a few video styles that you think will work with your target audience.

7. Decide on a persona that will characterize your work on YouTube.

8. Plan on developing a pipeline of videos, not just one.

9. Decide how you're going to get your videos completed and invest in that plan.

10. Consider partnering with vloggers to help share your story.

11. Decide whether you're going to use an on-screen format or an off-screen format for your primary video work.

12. Set up your YouTube channel.

13. Upload your first video.

14. Launch your new YouTube channel by cross-promoting it with your other marketing channels.

15. Determine whether a skills-based contest will work with your target market, and if so, launch one.

16. For charities, consider the powerful advantages of using YouTube as an engagement tool.

17. Identify the places you want to drive traffic to and determine how you'll use YouTube to drive it.

18. Learn to evaluate success using analytics.

19. Explore the YouTube advertising program options.

20. Ensure that you have a Call-to-Action overlay on each of your videos to help boost your traffic results.

21. If it's right for you, explore the monetization options and consider how you can make money by publishing videos.

I wish you all the best in your YouTube marketing efforts.

Index

About the Author

Jason G. Miles is the bestselling author of the Power Book series, a collection of books dedicated to providing exceptional content for work-at-home marketers. His third book in the series, *Email Marketing Power*, is an Amazon number one bestseller in the e-commerce category. His second book in the series, *Craft Business Power*, is an Amazon number one bestselling book in the e-commerce and web marketing categories. His first book in the series, *Pinterest Power*, is also an Amazon bestseller.

In 2008, Jason cofounded Liberty Jane Clothing with his wife, Cinnamon, and serves as the company's chief marketer. To date, Liberty Jane Clothing has had over 300,000 digital guidebooks downloaded from its e-commerce website. It is a thriving small business. Learn more at http://www.libertyjaneclothing.com.

Jason teaches marketing in the School of Business Management at Northwest University. He was formerly the senior vice president of advancement at Northwest University, where he led the marketing, fundraising, and human resources teams. In 2013, he retired in order to work full-time with his wife and to write.

Jason also leads an active coaching practice and loves helping entrepreneurs go from concept to cash. In 2012, he worked with over 1,250 small business owners to launch or grow their new businesses. As a frequent conference speaker and workshop leader, Jason leads marketers in exploring practical ways to leverage social media. He holds a graduate degree in business as well as undergraduate degrees in business and biblical studies. More information is available at http://www.youtubemarketingpower.com. You can follow Jason on Instagram at @mrjasonmiles and on his blog at http://www.marketing onpinterest.com.